Lake City Hiking

Lyndon J. Lampert

WESTERN REFLECTIONS
PUBLISHING COMPANY®

ISBN: 978-1-937851-48-4

Printed in the United States of America

Revised version of the original 1997 printing
by Golden Stone Press.

Cover photograph: Hiking to Uncompahgre
Peak by Allison Stewart.

Western Reflections Publishing Company
P. O. Box 1149
915 N. Highway 149
Lake City, Colorado 81235

www.westernreflectionspublishing.com
(970) 944-0110

CONTENTS

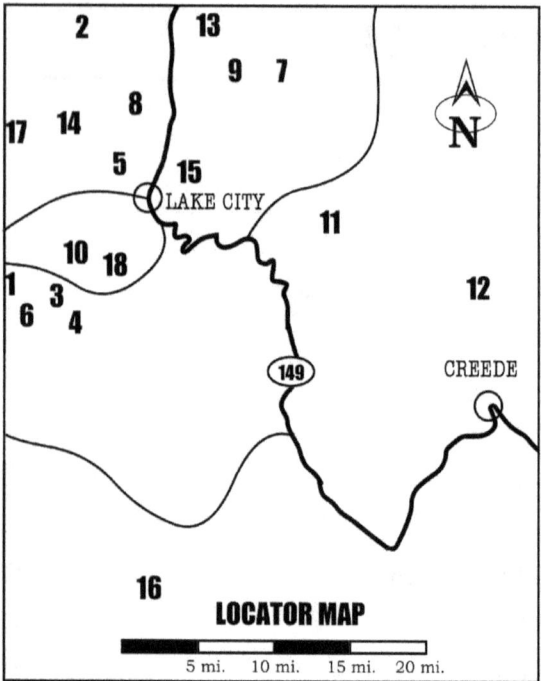

LOCATOR MAP

5 mi. 10 mi. 15 mi. 20 mi.

1 American Basin	**10** Redcloud Peak
2 Big Blue Creek	**11** Rough Creek
3 Black Wonder Gorge	**12** San Luis Peak
4 Cataract Gulch	**13** Skunk Creek
5 Crystal Lake	**14** Uncompahgre Peak
6 Handies Peak	**15** Waterdog Lake
7 Hidden Lake	**16** Weminuche Pass
8 Independence Gulch	**17** Wetterhorn Peak
9 Powderhorn Lakes	**18** Williams Creek

INTRODUCTION

This book is a compilation of hiking trails that first appeared in the author's publication, The *Lake City Outdoor Journal*, from 1987 until 1991. This guide retains those descriptions largely intact, with updated changes made where necessary. No attempt has been made to be comprehensive; the hikes herein are simply a sampling of some of the best to be found in the area.

Lake City hiking is mountain hiking at its finest, with trails available to those of all skill levels. Mountain hiking involves some particular hazards, however, and all hikers should be aware of what difficulties may await them on any trail described in this book.

ALTITUDE

No one should attempt any lengthy hiking in the Lake City area without a reasonable acclimation period. For those arriving from elevations of less than 5,000 feet, three days of light activity are usually enough to acclimate to hiking at all elevations in the San Juans. Drinking plenty of water and consumption of antacids may help speed acclimation.

ROUGH TRAILS

Although trail maintenance is carried out on a regular basis, hikers should expect sections of many trails to be rocky, steep, muddy, wet and/or snowy. Footwear with solid ankle support and good traction is vital, as is a reasonable degree of physical fitness. Whether you are on the Williams Creek Trail or Wetterhorn Peak, watch your step!

MOUNTAIN WEATHER

Nothing changes as quickly as mountain weather, and the confined nature of valleys makes it very difficult to see foul weather that may be closing in. It is not unusual, even in the summer, to experience blazing sun, wind, rain, sleet, hail, and snow on a single day hike.

Two tips will help you adequately deal with mountain weather. First, start early in the day. From July 1 through August, the weather generally deteriorates as the day progresses.

Thunderstorms and severe lightning can be a real hazard most afternoons. Thus, a good rule of thumb is to plan on being off any exposed summit or ridge by noon throughout the summer.

Second, hike prepared for variable weather. Take layers that are wind and rainproof, and don't forget a warm hat. Also, always carry adequate means to start a fire if necessary. It is foolhardy to hike in the mountains without a daypack equipped to meet whatever weather the day may serve up.

CRITTERS

The most threatening animal that Lake City hikers face is the Rocky Mountain wood tick. These are most common in brushy areas in May and June, and then decrease in abundance as the summer wears on. They can carry serious disease, so use tick repellent and check your clothes and hair often.

Giardia lamblia is a parasite that lives in many of our streams, and can cause protracted abdominal illness if ingested. Do not drink untreated stream or lake water; carry a filter or treat water with iodine.

Larger animals, such as black bears and mountain lions, pose almost no threat to hikers, and especially not if they are given their distance when spotted.

BECOMING LOST OR INJURED

Most of the trails in this book are well marked and travelled. If you're hiking in unfamiliar territory, though, it is a good idea to carry a topographic map and compass and know how to use them. If you do become genuinely disoriented, you are usually better off to retrace your steps or stay put rather than to press on into more unfamiliar territory. Always let someone know where you plan to hike and when you plan to return.

Each hiking party should have a basic first aid kit available. This will be adequate for minor injuries, but the best preparation may be to hike in groups of three or more. Then, if one is injured, one person can remain to render aid, while the other goes for help.

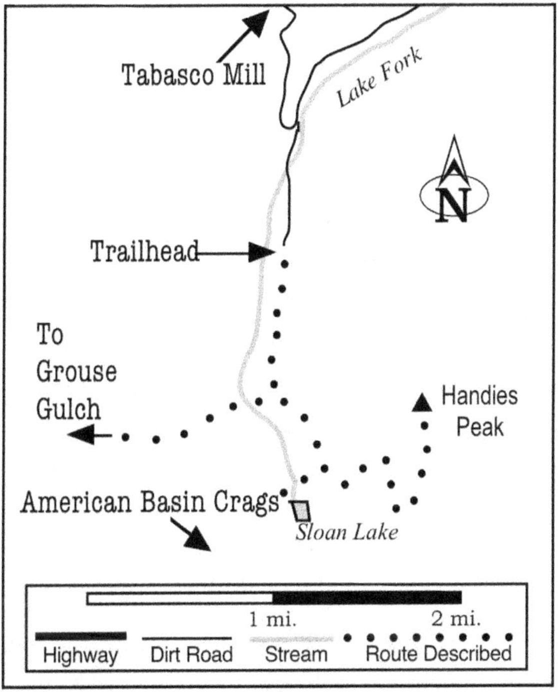
Tabasco Mill
Lake Fork
Trailhead
To Grouse Gulch
Handies Peak
American Basin Crags
Sloan Lake
1 mi.
2 mi.
Highway
Dirt Road
Stream
Route Described

1 American Basin

Is there any place in the San Juans as beautiful as American Basin? It's a tough question. Yankee Boy Basin above Ouray, Navajo Lake not far from Telluride, Chicago Basin in the Needles all spring to mind as scenic contenders.

However, while they may equal the sheer grandeur of American Basin, they surely do not exceed it. Here, compressed into only about three square miles are all those things that great mountains are supposed to have.

First, this is high country—some of the highest in the United States. Here earth meets sky in a grand fashion, a place where you can reach out and touch the clouds. Virtually all of the basin lies above timberline, stretching from elevations of 11,400´ to over 14,000´ on the slopes of Handies Peak, which forms its eastern wall. Everywhere in the basin one has the feeling of being very near the top of the San Juans, which is nearly true.

American Basin is also blessed with an enchanting combination of ruggedness and gentleness. The south wall of the basin is dominated by the precipitous American Basin Crags, the highest of which reaches 13,806´, and all of which drop in sheer cliffs to the basin floor. The sawtooth skyline formed by the crags has graced many a vacation slide show, not to mention innumerable postcards and calendars. The crags are especially spectacular when dusted by snow early or late in the season.

Though having its share of real ruggedness, American Basin also has a gentle side, contrasting sharply with the crags above. The floor of the basin is rolling and inviting, carpeted by lush grass and vegetation. Here sheep may graze and hikers laze under a brilliant summer sun.

Attractions of water are here, too. Early in the season, every gulch seems filled with a noisy cascade, lending the perfect audio touch to the scene. While there are no Yosemite-class waterfalls here, there are enough to complement the scene without stealing the show. And for those who are convinced that great mountain places simply must include a lake, American Basin offers Sloan Lake, right under the crags, and home to some sizable but wary cutthroat trout.

And still there's more in this amazing basin! Anyone who has been to American Basin in the summer immediately associates it with one of the best places to see alpine wildflowers anywhere. In a good year, acres and acres of larkspur, paintbrush, daisies, columbine, and dozens of other varieties of flowers paint the floor of the basin with glorious color. At this altitude, summer is extremely short, and the flowers seem to work extra hard to compress as much beauty into as small a span of time as possible!

Finally, if all this hasn't been enough, American Basin also offers much of interest to the history buff. Prospectors probably trickled into the basin from the Silverton side as early as the 1860s, but in the 1870s, things really boomed. Hopeful mining camps named Whitecross, Argentum, and Tellurium sprouted in nearby Burrows Park, and several mines were located within American Basin itself. The remains of the famed Tobasco Mill are just north of the basin along the road to Cinnamon Pass. Today other relics of this era are evident at several places in the basin in the form of mine openings and old roads, generally unobtrusive enough to be fascinating sidelights rather than offensive eyesores.

To reach American Basin drive from Lake City past Lake San Cristobal on the road to Cinnamon Pass for a total distance of about twenty-three miles. En route you'll negotiate the notorious Shelf Road (not for weaving drivers) and pass through the meadows of Burrows Park. Most high-clearance automobiles can make this trip with little difficulty thanks to considerable road improvements by Hinsdale County. Where the sign indicates the American Basin turnoff at a switchback at the foot of Cinnamon Pass, turn left and look for a parking place if you don't have four wheel drive; those who do can proceed about a mile further into the very heart of the basin.

The list of options of things to do in American Basin is at least as long as its list of attractions. An obvious thing to do in the summer is to stroll around the valley floor, admiring the wildflower show. See how many varieties you can identify and you can stay busy photographing all day long! In recent years, sheep grazing has been more tightly controlled in the basin, making the show excellent all summer long.

Those desiring a longer hike into the basin can't do much better than to set their sites on Sloan Lake, about two miles from the turnoff. The trail is obvious, and is also the most popular approach route to Handies Peak. Before the trail tackles Handies' south ridge, it takes you by the lake just under the crags at 12,900´. This is a steady climb, and you'll gain 1,500´ in less than two miles, but stopping frequently to enjoy American Basin's delights will take your mind off of your pounding heart and heaving lungs.

Along the way watch for the remnants of the silver rush. Prospectors here undoubtedly swore by the old adage, "a good silver mine is found above timberline ten times out of nine." High in the basin just below the lake you'll be able to look north and easily see the characteristic U-shape of this glacially carved basin. Also, here and there you'll see exposed outcroppings of bedrock smoothed by tons of glacial ice.

Sloan Lake itself is a beauty, a very blue sapphire set among the feet of the rock glaciers streaming north from the crags. If you're fishing, don't plan on ice being fully off the lake for certain until the middle of July. Also, don't plan on camping here without adequate equipment for dealing with the often extreme above-timberline conditions.

For those who feel barely exerted by the hike to Sloan Lake, it is only another mile to the northeast up the well-defined trail to the summit of 14,048´ Handies Peak. Or, there is another trail leading out of the basin to the west to overlook Grouse Gulch and the Animas River country north of Silverton.

I suppose if I had to single out one "must see" for the first time visitor to the San Juans, American Basin would have to be it. Its beauty does make it a bit crowded at times, but amongst its rolling meadows and spacious mountainsides is plenty of room to find your own private piece of this mountain paradise. Cherish this basin the best you can—you probably won't find another one like it in a lifetime.

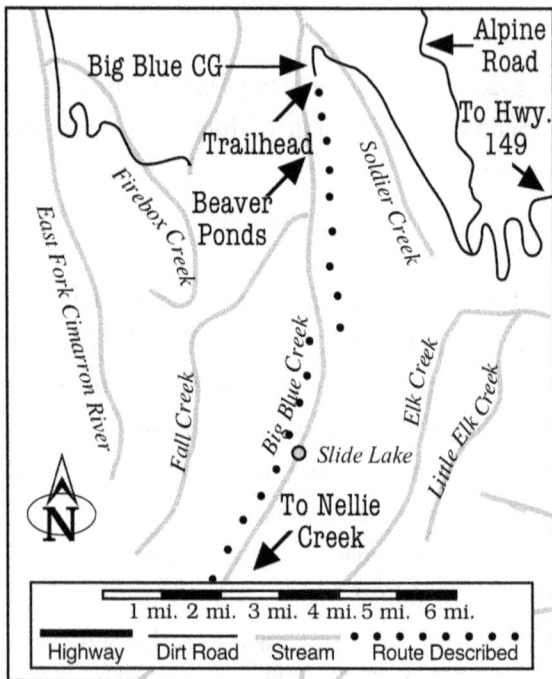

Map legend:

1 mi.	2 mi.	3 mi.	4 mi.	5 mi.	6 mi.
Highway	Dirt Road	Stream	Route Described		

2 Big Blue Creek

High above the chasm of Elk Creek, the Alpine Plateau Road clings to the mountainside for dear life. The view from the road is sheer. Formidable. Intimidating. At this point, the terrain is the West at its rugged finest, and anything but friendly. Amazing as it seems though, in a strange twist so characteristic of the varied Rockies, scarcely two miles from the imposing Elk Creek Canyon lies another, very different drainage. This is the Big Blue Valley-as gentle as Elk Creek Canyon is steep, as broad as Elk Creek Canyon is narrow, as friendly as Elk Creek Canyon is intimidating. Welcome to the astonishing West, and welcome to Big Blue Creek, a place to spend a day, a week, or a lifetime experiencing the gentle Rockies.

Big Blue Creek is an extremely long drainage, flowing for about thirty miles from its headwaters on the north flank of Uncompahgre Peak to its terminus in Morrow Point Reservoir at the famed Curecanti Needle. Though the landmarks at its beginning and end are classic examples of rugged Rocky Mountain grandeur, the Big Blue Valley itself remains anomalously gentle, a quiet intermission in the midst of an exciting mountain drama. The valley, simply called "The Blue" locally, is an ideal destination for the day hiker, the backpacker, the camper, the wildlife lover, and the fisherman alike. With plenty of elbow room, many folks can enjoy their favorite outdoor activity without rubbing shoulders with one another.

Despite its length, very few roads provide access to the Big Blue. U. S. Highway 50 crosses it near the stream's plunge into the Black Canyon, but the sole other public road reaching the valley is the Alpine Plateau Road which climbs from Colorado 149 eleven miles north of Lake City. This road (usually open June through November) snakes its way five miles up the mountainside and high above Elk Creek, crests Soldier Summit, and then drops on the other side for six more miles to the Alpine Guard Station and the Big Blue Campground. Using care, most vehicles can negotiate this road without trouble, but trailers are not advised. High clearance vehicles can continue another mile upstream past the campground to the road's end at the boundary of the Uncompahgre Wilderness. Whether spending a day or a week on the Blue, the campground is a logical place to headquarter. Tables and pit toilets are available in the small campground but there is no water, so you'll have to bring your own or boil water from the creek. Though popular in the height of summer, Big Blue Campground is seldom really crowded and you should be able to locate a vacant site or two almost anytime.

The Big Blue Valley offers a surprising number of interesting features in the immediate vicinity of the campground. Several beaver ponds just across the road are super places for kids to fish and to watch for a beaver or two. The best time to look for these animals is near dusk, when they can be seen swimming in the ponds or perhaps feeding and preening on shore. If you're quiet and very careful you may be able to approach quite close, but be forewarned that it doesn't take much to cause a beaver to disappear in a quick dive and thunderous slap of its tail!

An unusually large talus slope immediately to the north of the campground is another good place for an impromptu nature study. Here the geologic processes of weathering can be seen on a large scale, and it can be enjoyable to see how many forms of life you can discover on the barren-looking rock field. If you're here in the summer, one lifeform you're certain to see is the marmot, which for some reason seems less shy in the Big Blue Valley than almost anywhere else in the Lake City area. Perhaps, `a la Yellowstone bears, they have learned that campers make great neighbors!

Though it is certainly worthwhile to spend some time exploring around the campground, to really appreciate all the Big Blue has to offer you'll need to do some day hiking or backpacking. An excellent trail runs the entire length of the Big Blue Valley on National Forest land, and in stunning contrast to most San Juan trails, the Big Blue Trail is relatively gentle. In fact, in some places it is down-right level!

One good day hike is to walk downstream from the Alpine Guard Station for about three miles to where the National Forest land ends at a well-signed fence. This is a fine trip on an easy trail and traverses grassy meadows most of the distance. In the summer, watch for bluebirds, swallows, and red-tailed hawks. Deer can often be seen in the early morning coming to the creek for water. I once spooked a young buck while threading my way through the maze of willows near the stream from a distance of about three yards. I'm still not sure who was spooked more!

Those desiring longer hikes or backpacking will definitely want to explore the Big Blue upstream from the campground. The sky is the limit on hiking here, from short day hikes to backpacks of twenty miles or more deep within the Uncompahgre Wilderness.

The first few miles of trail above the road's end wind through lovely aspen groves above the creek to the east. Here and there impressive volcanic spires tower above the valley, reminiscent of the Wheeler Geological area. Along this stretch, too, you'll have good views of several active beaver ponds along Big Blue Creek's sinuous course. The winding nature of the stream indicates that Big Blue Creek is fairly "old" as streams go. The looping bends make for some good photos as well as create great pools for chunky brook trout. Incidentally, Big Blue Creek is one of the most consistent trout producers in the area, especially for those using a fly rod.

The trail crosses the stream about four miles up and then climbs another mile to one of the more popular destinations in the drainage, Slide Lake. Before reaching the lake, you'll puff your way up the sizable landslide that dammed up Big Blue Creek and created Slide Lake about forty years ago. The slide is a fascinating jumble of rubble, a miniature Slumgullion, and it is interesting to observe how life is regaining a foothold in this relatively recent "disaster area." Slide Lake itself is filling in rapidly and is not much to look at, but at times its fishing can be excellent.

Above Slide Lake, the trail steepens somewhat and continues three more miles through mixed woods and meadows to timberline and an absolutely awesome view of Uncompahgre Peak. If backpacking, you'll certainly want to camp here if for no other reason than the view! The upper Big Blue deserves a few days of exploration itself, with its alpine flowers, elk, pikas, and solitude. Those only desiring to explore the upper Blue can also reach it by a trail that climbs over the ridge from Nellie Creek.

Whether you spend a day or a week exploring the Big Blue Valley, you'll probably return. The gentle West, after all, is a rare treat well worth coming back to.

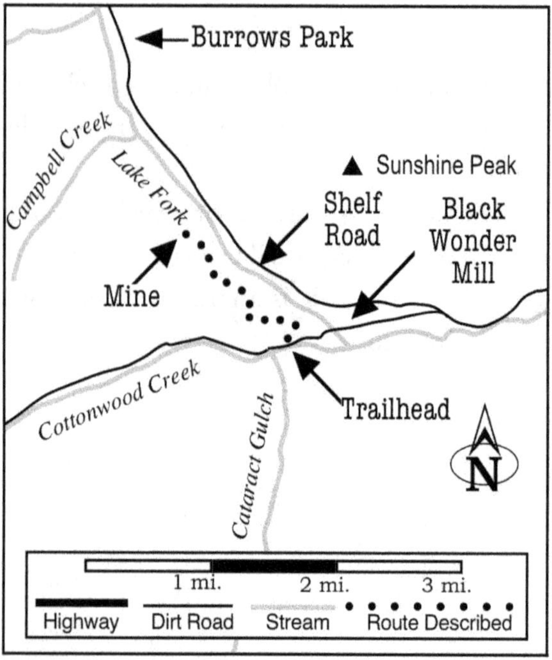
Burrows Park
Campbell Creek
Lake Fork
Sunshine Peak
Shelf Road
Black Wonder Mill
Mine
Cottonwood Creek
Trailhead
Cataract Gulch
N
1 mi.
2 mi.
3 mi.
Highway
Dirt Road
Stream
Route Described

3 Black Wonder Gorge

Some places are better visited from a distance. The Black Wonder Gorge, a spectacular two-mile gash in the bedrock of the San Juans, may well be one of those places. Although seen by thousands each year, probably less than a handful of folks annually venture anywhere into its depths, and it is a virtual certainty that no one has ever traversed its entire length at stream level. The gorge is a place you appreciate precisely for its inaccessibility—somehow it is simply good to know that places exist untamed and untamable, and the Black Wonder Gorge remains a small remnant of the San Juans as they once were.

Yet, as rugged as the gorge is, one obscure and moderately challenging trail gives the adventuresome hiker an excellent sampling of its many attractions. The Black Wonder Gorge is not named as such on any map, but derives its unofficial name from the famous Black Wonder millsite at its lower end. The gorge stretches from the old townsite of Sherman on the Upper Lake Fork of the Gunnison to the lower end of Burrows Park, about two or three miles upstream. In between is a canyon of up to 4,000 feet deep, one spectacular waterfall, and dozens of wild whitewater rapids. Simply stated, Black Wonder Gorge is a wild San Juan canyon at its best.

Many jeepers headed to or from Cinnamon Pass on the notorious Shelf Road have peered into the depths of Black Wonder Gorge, but in all probability most of them, anxious to proceed to flatter terrain, have not paused long enough above the gorge to fully appreciate its beauty. Fortunately, for those willing to hike a bit, a better option exists for enjoying the gorge than crawling along the Shelf Road behind a string of others doing the same thing. Directly across the gorge from the Shelf Road climbs another road, overgrown and closed to vehicles, but a road which offers the day hiker far better views into the canyon, no cliff side drop-offs, and an abundance of historical and natural features.

To reach the trailhead for the "other" road, drive to the townsite of Sherman, about fifteen miles above Lake City via County Roads 30 and 35. County Road 35 bears left just before the Cinnamon Pass road climbs a steep hill and becomes the Shelf Road. Take 35 for about another mile, passing the Black Wonder Mill ruins and crossing the Lake Fork on a good bridge. Shortly after crossing the river, you'll come to a BLM outhouse and parking area on the right. To avoid crossing private property, you'll need to climb directly up the hill to the north of the outhouse for a ways (no trail). After passing some rocky outcrops and climbing through some small grassy meadows, you'll intersect the Black Wonder Gorge trail (actually an old road) angling uphill from your right.

In the first half-mile or so, you'll gain most of the elevation of the trip, so take your time and enjoy the expansive view of the cottonwood-filled Sherman townsite below. As the trail climbs the ridge between Cottonwood Creek and the Lake Fork, you can almost hear the brakes grinding on the ore wagons that once descended here. This well-built road was constructed to serve a mine at the time of Sherman's boom, probably in the 1880s. Today it remains in relatively good condition, save for the young aspen trees that are poking up here and there. Avalanche activity was heavy in the gorge in 2019, however, so avalanche debris may cover parts of the trail, making it more challenging to negotiate.

Before you cross the top of the ridge into the Black Wonder Gorge, be sure to notice the green cradle of Cataract Gulch directly to the south. From near one switchback, you'll actually have a better view of the stair-stepping Cataract Gulch waterfalls than from Cataract Gulch itself! Cataract Gulch is a fine example of a hanging valley; that is, a valley that drops off very steeply at its lower end due to the gouging action of a large glacier in the Cottonwood Creek drainage. When the glacier disappeared, upper Cataract Gulch was left "hanging," and is much gentler in gradient than its lower portion.

After about one-half mile, the road breaks into a small clearing near the top of the ridge. Here you'll notice other effects of glacial action—several moderately large sections of exposed bedrock rounded by the passing ice.

Continue climbing, and at the second switchback you'll be at another small clearing on the very top of the ridge, and very near one of the highlights of the trip. At this point the thundering of the Lake Fork below is obvious, but the river is invisible. Leave the trail for a short distance here, carefully making your way to the very edge of Black Wonder Gorge. Far below in the narrow depths of the gorge is an unnamed forty-foot waterfall, entirely unseen by the thousands of jeepers that pass on the other side of the valley. Here the gorge is so narrow that it reminds me much of Box Canyon Falls near Ouray. At one point just above the waterfall, the gorge walls actually touch each other. An enticing green pool lies at the base of the falls, but even a fanatic fisherman would also have to be a technical rock climber in order to reach it!

Shortly after crossing the ridge, the road turns up the valley of the Lake Fork and moderates a bit. Here, in the mixed aspen, spruce, and Douglas Fir woods, is a good section in which to see many wildflowers. Most of these are dry-ground loving species such as red columbine, daisies, strawberries, Jacob's ladder, and heart-leaved arnica, but in at least one grove, a great number of white violets with blossoms the size of pennies can be discovered.

Not long after the violet garden, a view opens up directly across the gorge to the Shelf Road, and well below it, the shattered remains of a wooden flume. The flume once carried water for power generation at the Black Wonder Mill, and by the looks of things, must have been a real nightmare to construct! From this side of the gorge, the entire route of the flume may be spotted, while jeepers on the Shelf Road receive only a glimpse of it where it crosses a suspension bridge over a narrow chasm.

After about 1.5 miles, the road comes to its reason for existence—the remains of an interesting outside-framed structure that was once a miner's home. Appropriately, you may come across the hermit thrush here as well, a robin-like bird whose song sounds unforgettably like a melodious flute. Another quarter mile and some steep switchbacks brings you to a quartz-sprinkled tailings pile at the edge of an avalanche run. Snow from last winter's slides will usually be left in this run until late in the summer, and it's a good bet that this was one mine that didn't operate in the winter! The entrance to the mine itself has collapsed, but a lone piece of twisted rail bears testimony of extensive workings underground.

The magnitude of Black Wonder Gorge is better appreciated from the mine than anywhere else on the trip. Behind you, above the avalanche chute, a craggy unnamed summit reaches above 13,400′. Across the gorge, the cliffs and talus slopes of Sunshine Peak top out at 14,000′. Between the peaks and thousands of feet below them are the rapids and falls of the Lake Fork as it slashes its way through the gorge. As you ponder the immensity of the view, take a minute to watch for jeeps snaking along the Shelf Road, now well below you on the other side of the gorge, and ponder whether you'd rather be seeing Black Wonder Gorge from the back seat of a jeep on a bumpy road or from the grassy mountainside where you're seated now. Once you've seen Black Wonder Gorge from "the other side," the answer will be obvious.

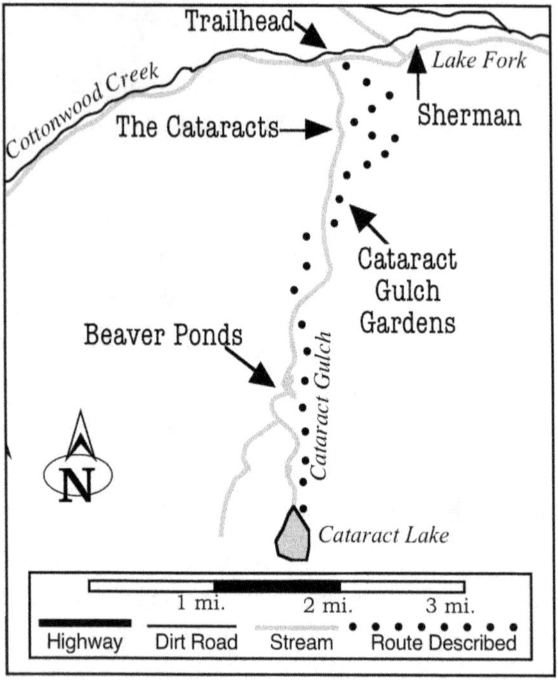
Trailhead
Cottonwood Creek
Lake Fork
Sherman
The Cataracts
Cataract Gulch Gardens
Beaver Ponds
Cataract Gulch
N
Cataract Lake
1 mi.
2 mi.
3 mi.
Highway
Dirt Road
Stream
Route Described

4 Cataract Gulch

If your idea of the perfect Rocky Mountain day hike includes the ingredients of a soaring views, a serene lake above timberline, cascade upon cascade of icy water, and wildflowers galore, then you should consider Cataract

Gulch the next time you get an itch to see the San Juans on foot. I know of very few other day hikes in the area that offer so much variety and beauty in so few miles as the Cataract Gulch Trail between Sherman and Cataract Lake.

As gorgeous as the Cataract Gulch Trail is, potential hikers should be aware that this is one of the more demanding day hikes in the area. The trail climbs steeply for about two thirds of the distance to the lake, and totals 2,450′ of elevation gain in only a little over four miles. Thus, a round-trip to the lake and back in a single day is demanding on virtually every hiker, and all but impossible to the unacclimated or ill-conditioned. The good news, though, is that Cataract Gulch offers many delights along its entire length, and shorter hikes only as far up the trail as you desire are amply rewarding.

The lower terminus of the Cataract Gulch trail is near the old townsite of Sherman, about sixteen miles from Lake City on County Road 30, the Cinnamon Pass approach. About one-half mile beyond the bridge over the Lake Fork, look for the Cataract Gulch Trail sign on your left. Here there is ample parking as well as several very good sites for establishing an overnight base camp if so desired.

The beginning of the Cataract Gulch Trail is not nearly as exciting as it used to be. In the "old days" (the early 1980s), the hiker was faced immediately with a frigid crossing of Cottonwood Creek, which early in the season could be running very high. Presently, however, a makeshift log bridge permits any hiker with even a modest sense of balance to cross to the other side high and dry. Lest the traditionalist hiker should feel cheated by this amenity, however, a couple of unavoidable stream wadings remain a few miles up the trail—just for nostalgia's sake.

Almost immediately, the Cataract Gulch Trail begins to climb. In only a short period of time the hiker is enveloped in a dark forest of Engelmann spruce and subalpine fir. Unfortunately, most of the mature spruce have been killed by a massive invasion of bark beetles in the 2010s. You can watch for signs of regeneration, though, in the form of seedling evergreens and aspen. Here, on the north slope of the Continental Divide, the shade is deep, and the air is cool. The last element will be more than welcome to any hiker, since the trail gains nearly 2,000 feet in the first two miles. Fortunately, though, the Cataract Gulch Trail is well-engineered, and long switchbacks moderate the strain of great elevation gain. Pause often here to listen for the rattling of a woodpecker or to admire the delicate beauty of a red columbine at trailside.

The first couple of miles of the trail are also the best from which to view the lovely cataracts for which the gulch is named. Whether the stream is in sight or not, the hiker is continually serenaded by the sounds of the nearby cascades. Now and then the trail passes close to the stream, and short spur hikes lead to some beautiful close-up views of a long series of whitewater falls and cascades. For many, a hike to the cataracts with a picnic lunch may be a perfect day hike in and of itself. Hikes of this nature can be as short as a mile and climb less than 1,000 feet.

Al about two miles up the gulch, the trail passes across some small avalanche paths near the stream. The walls above the gulch are truly spectacular here, soaring to bare cliffs on either side. The natural openings in the trees also permit a great view of the imposing mass of 14,000´ Sunshine Peak to the north, directly across the Lake Fork valley.

It is in this area, too, that the Cataract Gulch Gardens begin. I have hiked many, many, miles on many, many San Juan trails and I can honestly say that I have found no other place in these mountains that exceeds the luxurious profusion of flowering plant growth of the central portion of the Cataract Gulch Trail. Why the flowers grow so thickly and so tall here is no mystery, though. To begin with, the northern exposure of the gulch holds more moisture than south-facing slopes, but perhaps more importantly, the deeply incised gulch coupled with the constant spray from the cataracts traps moisture in and creates a naturally humid greenhouse. In the midst of this superabundant moisture, flowers like bluebells, monkshood, columbine, and many other species thrive. Like the cataracts, the trailside gardens also make an extremely worthwhile destination.

Not far from the gardens the trail passes right by an old mine shack and a small tailings dump. This mine was probably never profitable, but at least its owner had an appreciation of beauty! Above the mine, the trail climbs steeply toward perhaps the prettiest waterfall in the gulch. A good campsite or picnic site can be found just above the falls, very near one of the wading crossings of the stream (not nearly as large as Cottonwood Creek).

Once the falls are reached, the majority of the climbing will have been done, and the trail is steep only in places the remaining distance to Cataract Lake. The sudden moderating of the grade is a testament to Cataract Gulch's status as one of the finest "hanging valleys" in the area. This hanging valley was formed when a large glacier in the Lake Fork drainage scoured out the end of the original Cataract Gulch as it ground past it at right angles. This large glacier was thus responsible for the steep lower end of the gulch, while the gentle upper end "hangs above," retaining its original grade.

At about three miles up the trail, a small bowl filled with beaver ponds is reached. This, too, is an excellent day hike destination, especially for fishermen. While Cataract Lake often winterkills, these ponds never do, and often provide exceptional action for brook trout averaging nine to ten inches. The original Cataract Lake Trail passes close to the ponds, but winds through some brushy and swampy areas. The present trail climbs steeply up a bluff to the east of the ponds and tops out about 11,900′. From then on, it is gentle, above-timberline hiking for the remaining mile to Cataract Lake. This is a superb section in which to look for miniature alpine wildflowers and pikas and ptarmigan.

Cataract Lake finally shows itself at the head of a broad grassy basin just below the Continental Divide at mile 4.2. The unconditioned hiker will undoubtedly think it is much farther than this. Cataract Lake lies at 12,082′, and is about sixteen acres in extent. Historically, Cataract Lake has produced some of the biggest brook trout in the area (three to four pounds), but its unfortunate tendency to winterkill makes it an iffy fishing hole. Ask locally before you head here expecting to catch that trophy brookie.

Cataract Lake is of course the ultimate destination for a day hike up Cataract Gulch, but unless you start very early, don't expect to spend much time at the lake—thunderstorms at this elevation come shortly after noon and can be severe. Be equipped for rain, because at 12,000´ there are no trees to hide under! Even if the strenuous trip to the lake isn't possible for you, though, consider a shorter hike up Cataract Gulch, a trail where fascinating destinations seem to wait around every bend.

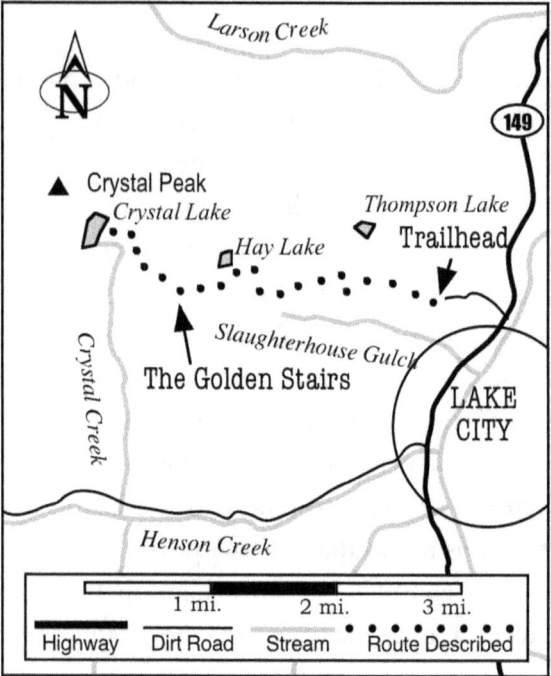

Larson Creek

N

▲ Crystal Peak
Crystal Lake

Thompson Lake
Trailhead

Hay Lake

149

Slaughterhouse Gulch

The Golden Stairs

Crystal Creek

LAKE CITY

Henson Creek

	1 mi.	2 mi.	3 mi.
Highway	Dirt Road	Stream	• Route Described

5 Crystal Lake

Choosing a favorite from among all of the alpine lakes in the Lake City area is no easy task, for each offers a unique charm impossible to compare with the others. However, I would be hard-pressed to argue with anyone who would want to place Crystal Lake at the top of their list.

An ideal alpine lake, in my highly subjective opinion, should first of all be a delight to behold, and Crystal Lake, complete with a wooded island tucked into one corner, is a real treat for the eye. Second, the ideal lake should have a stunning backdrop, and the rugged outline of Crystal Peak rising directly from the depths of the lake meets this obligation. Third, such a lake simply should have fish, and the fat brookies of Crystal Lake qualify easily.

For the sake of sheer laziness, the lake should not be too difficult to reach, and the fine Crystal Lake Trail, although a steady climb, is not unending torture for most people. Finally, campsites at such a lake should be wooded and level, an impossible requirement for almost every mountain lake in Colorado, but one met with liberality along Crystal Lake's eastern shore. Now that I've finally put all this in writing, I'm more convinced than ever that if you've never been to Crystal Lake, I must ask, "Why in the world not?"

The Crystal Lake Trail begins at the IOOF Cemetery, just north of Lake City. The turnoff is marked at the crest of the hill as Highway 149 leaves town. Drive this road (Balsam Drive) to the cemetery, or if you have four-wheel drive, another half-mile further up the mountain. Be forewarned that parking at the upper trailhead is extremely limited. Although this road was once drivable much further, a gate now stops motorized travel at 9,400´. For those who would like to reach Crystal Lake but still find four miles and 3,000 feet a bit daunting, consider contacting a local outfitter who can rent horses for the trip.

The trail begins in a grove of tall aspen, but soon emerges on a ridge above Slaughterhouse Gulch among some fine ponderosa pines. For the next mile or so you'll be treated to some bird's-eye views of Lake City and you can have some fun picking out houses you recognize, or more properly, roofs you recognize!

Soon the trail begins to climb through grassy meadows, and several newly-constructed switchbacks spare you from the former agonizing direct route up the mountainside. The grade is steady here but not excruciating.

About a mile up, the trail leaves the meadow and enters into aspen woods again, and the dominant sound from here to Hay Lake is the quiet rustling of leaves overhead, or if you're here in the autumn, the soft crunching of the yellow carpet beneath your feet. If flowers are in bloom, watch for heart-leaved arnica, aspen, daisies, and lupine.

In the vicinity of Hay Lake, about 2.5 miles and 2,300 feet above Lake City, the terrain grows considerably rockier, the remnants of a Slumgullion-type land movement that extends from Crystal Lake to the Riverside Subdivision on the north edge of Lake City. Here you'll have views of Cannibal Plateau to the east and the high country around Slumgullion Pass. Hay Lake, on the right side of the trail, is small and isn't much to look at, but fishermen may want to venture a cast or two into its murky water.

From Hay Lake to Crystal Lake, you'll climb about 700 feet in 1.5 miles—only moderately steep by San Juan standards. If the climbing gets wearisome, simply stop and enjoy the ever-expanding view, or see if you can spot a golden-crowned kinglet or Clark's nutcracker in the crowns of nearby spruce trees.

Not far above Hay Lake, the trail twists up a series of short, tight switchbacks called the Golden Stairs, and then levels off dramatically along the banks of an old irrigation ditch. Anyone who doubts that water in the West is as valuable as gold should consider the effort expended to construct this diversion ditch at such an unlikely location! The ditch is no longer used, but is a reminder of the intrepid lot of folks who lived here before and eked out a living from the land.

When the trail enters the impressive upper basin of Crystal Creek, you'll enjoy a spectacular view of the unnamed peaks at the head of Alpine Gulch and many of the other mountains that lie between Henson Creek and the upper Lake Fork of the Gunnison. If you're here early enough in the season (May or June) the contrast between the dry southern exposure of the Crystal Lake Trail here and the snow-laden northern basins of these peaks is simply amazing.

The trail levels out (finally) at 11,700′ in a wonderful large meadow just east of Crystal Lake, with 12,933′ Crystal Peak dominating the skyline. Only a few hundred yards more and you'll be in the woods at an old cabin on the shore of the lake itself. If you have only the afternoon to spend here, consider a walk around the lake, or perhaps a stroll through the many meadows to the northeast. If you haven't had enough climbing, an ascent of Crystal Peak via the north ridge is not too difficult, or you can probe around its base for the crystals for which the peak and lake are named. Fishing can be good with a fly and bubble or spinner, but as with all alpine lakes, may be temperamental. Perhaps the best idea of all is to come prepared to spend the night here, and then at your leisure you can do all of the above—who, after all, could possibly want to rush their experience of Lake City's near-perfect alpine lake?

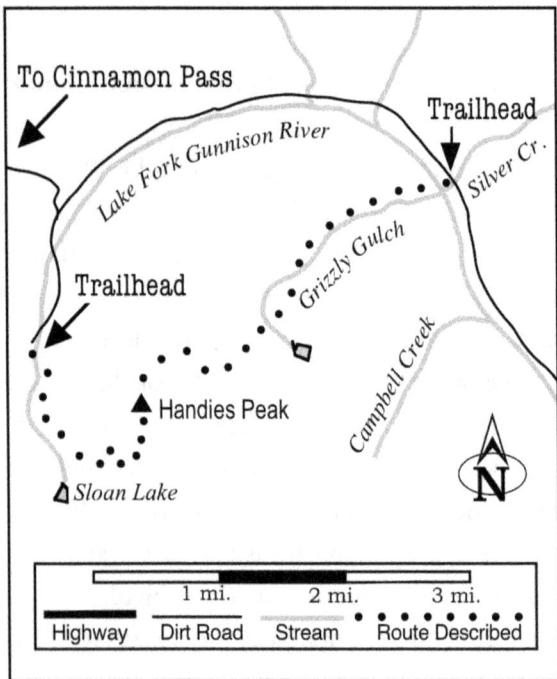

To Cinnamon Pass

Trailhead

Lake Fork Gunnison River

Silver Cr.

Trailhead

Grizzly Gulch

Campbell Creek

▲ Handies Peak

N

△ Sloan Lake

1 mi.	2 mi.	3 mi.
Highway	Dirt Road	Stream	Route Described

6 Handies Peak

Choosing an all-time favorite view is no easy matter, particularly in the spectacular San Juan Mountains. The vista from the crest of Engineer Pass, the San Miguel Range as seen from near Telluride, and the Sneffels Range from Ridgway all come immediately to mind. However, if I had to choose only one view to imprint in my memory for the remainder of my days, it would be the panorama from the summit of Handies Peak.

The bristling crags overlooking American Basin and the deep aquamarine of Sloan Lake treat the eye nearby, while a more distant gaze will take in the ragged Grenadiers and Needles Mountains near Silverton, Mount Sneffels, Uncompahgre and Wetterhorn, the La Garitas, Bristol Head … well, pretty much the entire glorious immensity of the San Juans!

And still the view continues! Studding the farthest horizon are the Grand Mesa, the West Elk Range, the Maroon Bells, portions of the Sawatch Range, and even the Sangre de Cristos across the San Luis Valley. All told, the climber atop Handies takes in 8,000 square miles of alpine grandeur at a single glance.

The view from Handies was the primary interest of the man who made its first recorded ascent, Franklin Rhoda. Rhoda was assistant topographer for Dr. Ferdinand V. Hayden's

United States Geological and Geographical Survey of the Territories, which undertook its monumental task of mapping the unmapped in 1873.

Mountain peaks were obvious choices for doing triangulation work, and a party headed by Rhoda ascended Handies in the summer of 1874. Since his work required a good deal of unwieldy equipment, Rhoda traveled "burro-back" to 13,000 feet, and finished the climb on foot. While Rhoda's was the first recorded ascent of the peak, he noted that it had surely been climbed by others before them, since they had seen prospect holes at the 13,500-foot level.

Mining began on Handies Peak in the early 1870s. The tiny community of Whitecross was established at the northeast foot of the mountain in the late 1870s, and mines were scattered among Burrows Park, American Basin, and Cinnamon Pass. Mines such as the Bonhomme, Champion, and Cracker Jack produced for a few years, but perhaps the operation best remembered was the Tobasco.

The Tobasco Mine was located on Cinnamon Pass, and was named for the famous meat sauce company that financed the operation. For a time, Handies Peak was called Tobasco Peak, but this fell from usage and the name reverted to "Handies," the original appellation recorded by Rhoda. Nothing, incidentally, is known of the person for whom Handies is named, though there is speculation that he was a San Juan pioneer of the 1870s.

The silver veins of Handies Peak were not rich, and since the 1920s there has been very little mining activity near the mountain. Handies is now once again the domain of the pika, the alpine sunflower, and the hiker. Handies is a great peak to start with for those interested in trying their legs and lungs on a 14,000´ peak. Few Fourteeners offer a more pleasant climb, and of course the view is second to none.

There are a couple of good approaches to the peak. The first, and most popular is via American Basin from the trail to Sloan Lake. Taking a four-wheel drive to the road closure will make Handies a climb of only about 2,600 feet in two miles. If you can get to American Basin before the sheep herds do, it will be a wonderful display of alpine wildflowers—so spectacular that you may just forget about climbing the mountain!

The second approach to Handies, and a personal favorite, is via Grizzly Gulch from the northeast. This route is longer and the elevation gain is about 1,000′ more, but I believe the extra effort is worth it. Grizzly Gulch is one of the best-kept hiking secrets in the Lake City area. Hiking up from the Burrows Park trailhead gives you a wilderness feeling almost immediately, and the beauty of the drainage easily equals that of American Basin.

The trail parallels a series of cascades to timberline, and then the valley opens up to a handsome view of the peak above acres and acres of spring green alpine meadows bursting with flowers. Above treeline, the remaining route up Handies is cairn-marked and generally obvious as it heads far up the basin and then curls around to Handies' north ridge. If you don't climb the peak, it is worthwhile to at least hike to timberline on the Grizzly Gulch Trail. Now that I've let out the secret of this hidden valley I may regret it, but somehow I don't think so—places like Grizzly Gulch are meant to be shared.

A climb of Handies is indeed strenuous physical labor, but should be little problem for anyone properly equipped and who can hike several miles on mountain trails at high altitude. No matter how high on the peak you ascend, if you choose a summer's day when the flowers are in their glory and the sky is a dazzling blue, your day on Handies Peak will be one of the highlights of your summer. And if you do push on to the summit, the view will be with you for a lifetime.

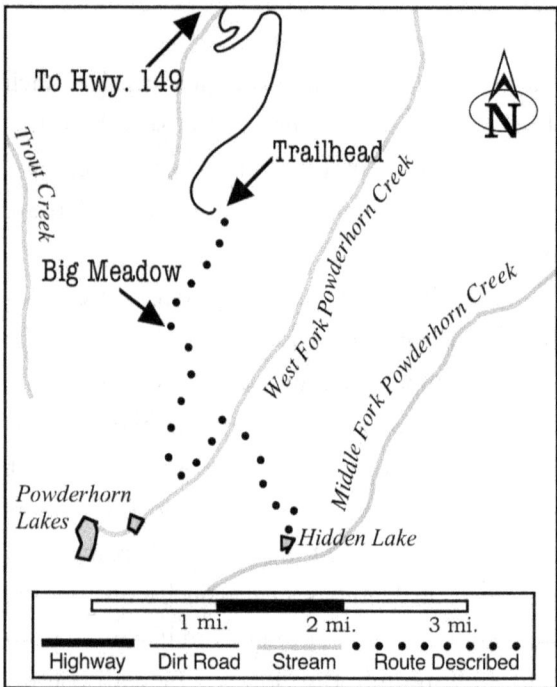

7 Hidden Lake

There's no doubt about it—any lake with a name like "Hidden" simply begs to be found. For several years, the name alone was sufficient to stir up the explorer in me. Unanswered questions nagged at my curiosity, such as, just where is this mysterious lake, why is it hidden, and most important, are there any fish in it? After all, I reasoned, it only figures that Hidden Lake simply must have great fishing.

There comes a point beyond which no human being can bear such unsolved mysteries, and for me, that point arrived in the summer of 1987. Donning hiking boots and daypack, and with fly rod in hand, I set out to find the elusive Hidden Lake. Before leaving my front door, I faced a significant problem—neither Hidden Lake nor the trail to it was indicated on any of my topographic maps. So much the better! The mystery was thickening at every step.

Knowing the general location of the lake, I was able to narrow its location to two possible choices on the topographic map. Here again arose another difficulty. Both of these bodies of water appeared as dry lakes on the map—not at all my idea of good fishing holes. By this time, however, I had learned to take such inexplicable mysteries in stride, and full of expectancy, confidently clambered into the cab of my `66 Dodge.

The shortest approach to Hidden Lake is from Highway 149 about twenty five miles north of Lake City. Just beyond the Sapinero Cutoff road, take the next dirt road to the right, marked "Powderhorn Primitive Area 10 miles." It's a long ten miles, as the road is rough and slow, but is usually passable for two-wheel drive vehicles. Built for logging purposes, the approach road passes through numerous old timber cuts. It is a good road on which to watch for deer in the early morning, and perhaps a bear or two.

The trailhead for Hidden Lake, which is also the trailhead for Powderhorn Lakes, is located at about 11,000′ at the end of the road. Take some time to read the information on the sign, and sign the trail register. Registers provide valuable information concerning the use of the Primitive Area, and greatly assist search efforts should you become lost or injured.

From the parking area, the trail climbs gradually, winding through a forest of Englemann spruce and Subalpine fir for about two miles to one of the finest locations of the entire route, an expansive meadow nearly at timberline on the north shoulder of Calf Creek Plateau. It is a place made for a rest, so take time to check out the expansive view to the west looking down the Trout Creek drainage, or see how many species of wildflowers you can identify in the huge meadow. This meadow is also a drawing point for many species of wildlife, most notably elk. One day I was fascinated here watching a young coyote hunting mice or voles, apparently completely oblivious to my presence.

If you can tear yourself away from the beauty of the meadow, continue across it and down the trail back into the woods. Here the woods are wetter than the woods a mile or so back, so keep an eye open for wetland flower species, such as the marsh marigold. The trail continues generally downhill past a couple of small ponds, and finally enters another meadow, about two miles from the first meadow. Here you'll meet a trail coming up West Powderhorn Creek from your left. To reach Hidden Lake, turn off onto this trail, unless you want to take a short side trip to Lower Powderhorn Lake, only about a quarter mile upstream from this junction.

The trail down West Powderhorn Creek parallels the stream rather closely, beckoning the fisherman to cast into its tiny pools and runs. If you do, you'll find plenty of small brookies and a few cutthroats willing to give you a tussle. At about .3 miles below the trail junction, watch for an obvious sign with two arrows pointing to Hidden Lake. Fortunately, the arrows are both pointing the same direction! The Hidden Lake trail is not very distinct at this junction point, but if you hike toward the stream, in the direction of the arrows, you'll soon spot a surprisingly well-worn path on the other side of the creek.

Across the stream, the trail climbs rather steeply up the opposite side of the valley, through a couple of talus piles that are speckled with patches of columbine in the early summer.

After this short steep stretch, the trail tops out on a broad, nearly flat ridge which makes for great strolling. This, too, is a meadow area, and you'll need to keep an eye on the large rock cairns to stay on the route. When the trail dips back into the timber, you will notice a body of water below you—one of the two "dry" ones on the topo. "Is this Hidden Lake?" I asked myself as I peered into its tinged, sterile-looking waters. I sure hoped not, and moved on down the trail toward the only other possibility.

Fifteen minutes later, I had my answer. At the end of a long narrow meadow, I walked up to another small lake almost before I knew it was there. It could be nothing but the mysterious Hidden Lake. Protected by the forest, and not visible from any nearby high points, Hidden Lake can't be seen until you are nearly on its shore. The lake is not large, not more than two or three acres, but the clarity of its water is unsurpassed. In a moment, I had the answer to another question—there were trout in Hidden Lake. In minutes, my fly rod was assembled and I was casting to cruising fish.

The atmosphere of Hidden Lake is one of intimacy and solitude. Here was no spectacular alpine cirque or even a view of nearby peaks, just the quiet beauty of a pure body of water dimpled by an occasional lazy rise of a trout. It is a place in which you feel wonderfully alone. The shoreline was remarkably free from any sort of litter, indicating that those who visit Hidden Lake respect its beauty and wish to see it preserved.

When I returned to Lake City that evening, Hidden Lake was no longer a mystery to me. Instead, I felt as though I had just made a new friend—one who I would visit again. If you would like to make friends with Hidden Lake too, it is the "dry" lake indicated in Section 24, R 3W, T45N on the Powderhorn Lakes Quadrangle. The trail is about ten miles round-trip, and involves about 1,100 feet of elevation gain going in, and 700 feet coming out By the way, I did mention that there are trout in Hidden Lake, but I didn't say how large or what species they are. After all, there needs to remain something mysterious about Hidden Lake, doesn't there?

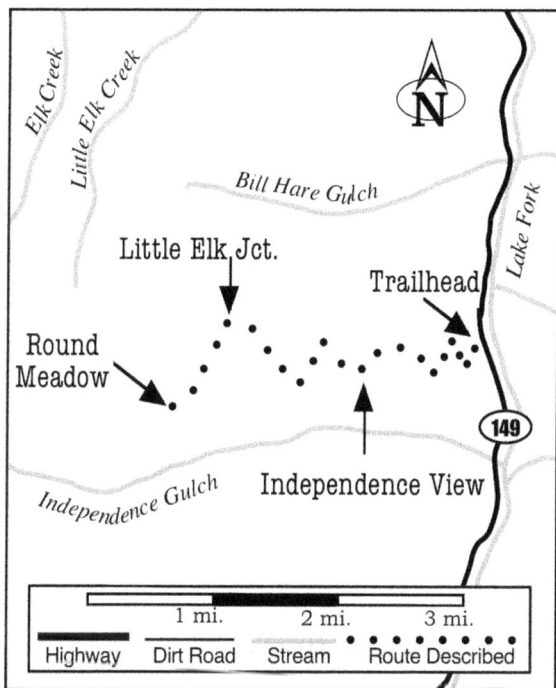

Elk Creek

Little Elk Creek

Bill Hare Gulch

Little Elk Jct.

Trailhead

Round Meadow

Lake Fork

149

Independence View

Independence Gulch

| 1 mi. | 2 mi. | 3 mi. |

| Highway | Dirt Road | Stream | Route Described |

8 Independence Gulch

Living in Lake City with its relative comforts of hot running water, electricity, and internet access, I sometimes forget just how close to untamed wilderness I really am. A hike up the Independence Gulch trail, though, erases any doubt that it is wilderness and not civilization that still reigns in Hinsdale County, and that places that seldom feel the tread of man exist but minutes from my front door.

The Independence Gulch trailhead is well marked at a broad pullout along Highway 149 in Baker Canyon, about six miles north of Lake City. Its proximity to Lake City makes it an excellent choice for a half-day trip, but hikers should be prepared for some steady hill climbing in the first mile and a half.

The trail immediately switchbacks up the side of Baker Canyon, thus not even permitting a gentle breaking-in stretch! However, hikers that are winded by these initial switchbacks can take some comfort in the fact that the remainder of the trail doesn't get much steeper than this (however, in the first 1.5 miles it isn't a whole lot gentler, either!) The trail begins solidly within the montane life zone, and the dominant tree for the first couple of miles is Douglas fir, with a few ponderosa pine and aspen adding variety. The trees are well-spaced here, due to the relatively low annual precipitation, and things feel "roomy." Where the trail levels out at a couple of too-brief stretches, look for patches of sagebrush and pause to inhale their intoxicating aroma.

The steady pull up the first half of the Independence Gulch Trail can be made somewhat more pleasant by watching for trailside flowers and birds. At this low elevation, expect to see lupine, scarlet gilia, penstemon, daisies, Indian paintbrush, and perhaps a few violets. At the higher elevations of the trail, you'll likely spot wild iris, heart-leaved arnica, and if you're exceptionally fortunate, perhaps even the rare calypso orchid. Birds that you might see anywhere on this trail include pine siskins, juncos, Cassin's finches, chickadees, ruby-crowned kinglets, hermit thrushes, and most colorful of all, western tanagers.

At about a mile up, the trail turns left in a pretty meadow flanked by three truly ponderous ponderosas and heads for a saddle. For a very short trip, this sagebrush-cloaked saddle is a good destination, but resist the temptation of short cutting down into Independence Gulch itself, just to the north. It's a severe bushwhack and ends on private land.

One-half mile more of steady climbing on good trail brings you to the Big Blue Wilderness boundary and an exposed ridge at about 9,400´. Here you'll have a fine view of Independence Gulch below. It could be called Independence Canyon, for it really is an impressive gorge, timbered and 600 feet deep here. You'll undoubtedly want to stop for a breather and some scenery-soaking.

From this point, the trail continues somewhat less steeply up long switchbacks that ascend the sagebrush-covered ridge to the west. Here you'll enjoy ever-expanding views of Cannibal Plateau, and a glimpse or two of the West Elk Mountains, far to the north.

After skirting through the woods on the north side of a rocky knob, the trail tackles a final few switchbacks and then tops out on a remarkably level hilltop I call The Table. The Table abruptly (and thankfully) ends the uphill climbing on this section of the trail. On the very top of The Table, you'll pass through a unique notch in a natural rock wall, and then stroll gently downhill.

At a point about 2.5 miles from the trailhead and 1,700 feet above it, the trail meets the Little Elk Trail in a small aspen meadow. The Little Elk Trail is even less-traveled than the Independence Gulch Trail, as it traverses unspoiled country to the north.

Just downhill from the Little Elk junction, the Independence Gulch Trail enters what I call The Grove of Giants, which contains some of the most massive aspen trees I have seen in the area. The trunks of some of these aspen approach two feet in diameter and lend a regal air to this part of the trail.

Shortly below The Grove of Giants, the trail crests a small ridge, and a large round meadow ringed by aspens appears below. This meadow is an excellent destination for a day hike, and ought to be spectacular when the aspens blaze golden yellow in the fall. The trail continues across the meadow, though, and soon turns up the creek on its way to meet the Larson Lakes Trail just above Larson Lakes. A side trip to the lakes, though, would add an additional six miles round-trip and 1,400 vertical feet—a very long day.

Independence Gulch is an excellent day hike for the early season, since much of the trail lies on south-facing slopes and it reaches only moderate elevations. It is also an excellent conditioner for winter-soft muscles and gives just enough of a taste of wilderness to get you hungering for more.

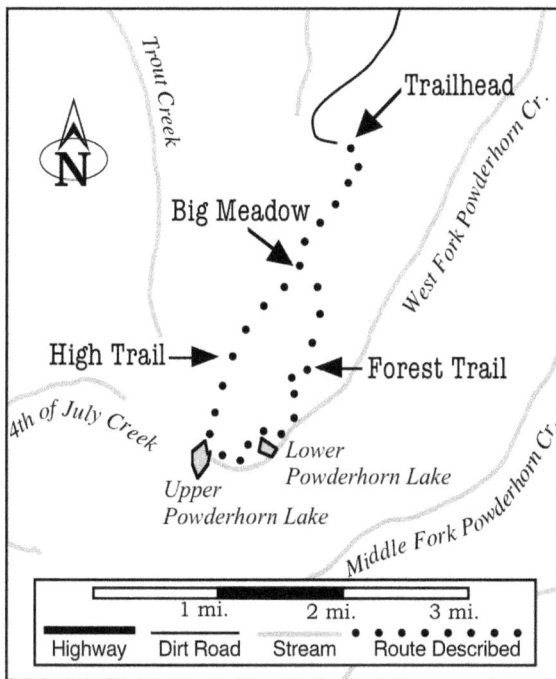

Map labels:
Trout Creek
Trailhead
West Fork Powderhorn Cr.
Big Meadow
High Trail→
←Forest Trail
4th of July Creek
Lower Powderhorn Lake
Upper Powderhorn Lake
Middle Fork Powderhorn Cr.

	1 mi.	2 mi.	3 mi.
Highway	Dirt Road	Stream	Route Described

9 Powderhorn Lakes

High mountain lakes are nearly always gems of rare beauty, and so when two are strung along the same chain, a truly exceptional piece of natural jewelry is created. Such is certainly the case of Upper and Lower Powderhorn

Lakes, two gems that are accessible by a moderate trail and that are attractive to the day hiker, backpacker, and fisherman alike. Tucked into a quiet corner of Lake City country, the lakes are not heavily visited and offer a great change of pace for those looking for some space in the increasingly crowded San Juans, especially for those who like to fish.

The Powderhorn Lakes nestle in a glacially-gouged basin, or cirque, on the northern edge of the high mesa called Calf Creek Plateau. Surrounded on three sides by cliffs, the only moderate approach to the lakes is from the north, and the hiker has a choice of two slightly different routes. A low route climbs moderately and offers the joys of quiet woodland hiking, while a high route climbs more steeply, but affords dramatic views of not only the lakes themselves, but also much of western Colorado. The hiker or horseback rider, then, can select his preference, or go in one way and return the other. Both routes require a bit of effort, but neither are difficult by San Juan standards. The most-used and shortest trailhead to Powderhorn Lakes is from the end of a ten mile dirt road that leaves Highway 149 about 24.5 miles north of Lake City, just east of the Sapinero Mesa Cutoff Road. A sign indicating the Powderhorn Primitive Area is the place you'll want to turn. This is a generally good (though slow) road passable in two-wheel drive unless it is very wet. In the course of the ten miles you'll climb from sagebrush country to well within the subalpine zone to the road's end and trailhead at about 11,200′.

The first 1.5 miles to Powderhorn Lakes is along the same trail regardless of whether you prefer the high route or the low route. In 1989 this first section of trail was entirely relocated from climbing fairly steeply up a hill to its present more moderate course along the hill's northern flank. For 1.5 miles this trail climbs through a mature spruce/fir forest, with only occasional glimpses through the heavy timber into the drainage of upper Indian Creek. Look for flowers like red columbine or heart-leaved arnica here, or watch for gray squirrels and woodpeckers.

At approximately mile 1.5, this trail breaks into a huge meadow at about 11,700. This meadow is a fine destination in its own right, complete with a great wildflower display and long views into the Trout Creek drainage to the northwest. In the early morning or late evening, you may also see elk grazing here.

If you can tear yourself away from this spot, though, here you'll next have the decision of which route to take to the lakes. The marked route is the lower route and swings across the meadow and back into the woods. The high route is not marked, but is discernible as a trail that ascends the broad ridge directly south of the meadow. If you are not comfortable with reading a topographic map or being off of clearly marked trails, the low route is your best choice.

The low route continues through the woods, alternately falling and climbing as it crosses several small drainages. At one point, you'll pass a placid woodland pond, where you might expect to spot a moose. The low route climbs fairly steeply at about mile three for a short bit, and then emerges in a meadow alongside some beaver ponds at West Powderhorn Creek. One-half mile and a small hill further upstream, the trail reaches Lower Powderhorn Lake.

Returning to the big meadow, the upper route follows one of several parallel sheep trails first through the meadow, and then above timber-line, generally near the crest of the broad ridge that sweeps down from Calf Creek Plateau. Choosing this route means that you'll climb an additional 300′ (600′ total if the high route is your choice both ways) over the low route, but many believe the extra effort is worth it.

As you ascend this gentle ridge, the view keeps expanding until it becomes almost too much to contain. At the high point you'll be standing at over 12,400′, and will be able to see, in but a turn of your head, the northern San Juans around Uncompahgre Peak, Alpine Plateau, Grand Mesa near Delta, the West Elk Mountains, the Maroon Bells near Aspen, and much of the rest of the Elk Range, the broad Gunnison Valley, most of the Sawatch Range between Monarch Pass and Taylor Park, the impressive bulk of Mount Ouray to the east, lonely Sawtooth Mountain nearer in the east, the La Garita Mountains, and on a clear day, even a portion of the Sangre de Cristo Mountains at the extent of your eastern horizon. In addition to the superb view, you'll also see numerous species of alpine wildflowers at your feet, and maybe even an elk or two grazing in the rolling meadows of Calf Creek Plateau.

As you near the crest of this ridge, watch for two man-sized rock cairns spaced fairly far apart. The trail passes between these two cairns and should become distinct once again after it passes over a small rock field or two. At this point both Powderhorn Lakes will be laid out below you in their splendor, like twin sapphires in a setting of native stone. It is possible to drop directly to Lower Powderhorn Lake from here, but a better route continues a bit further south and then drops fairly steeply to the upper lake.

Though the two lakes are within a half-mile of each other, at shoreline each presents quite a different appearance. The lower lake is smaller, about nine acres, and is set in a pleasant grassy hollow surrounded on three sides by woods. Campsites can be found in the woods, and the lake has a pleasant, sheltered appeal. Brook trout and cutthroat trout offer fairly consistent fishing here, averaging ten or eleven inches, with the brookies being more common. In addition, the West Fork of Powderhorn Creek has very good fishing for both species, especially for fly fishermen.

The setting of the upper lake is much more dramatic than the lower. It is bordered on three sides by steeply rising cliffs and bare talus slopes, and lies right at timberline, at nearly 11,900´. Upper Powderhorn is also a much larger body of water, comprising twenty-seven acres—one of the largest alpine lakes in the area. After visiting most of the lakes in the Lake City vicinity, I rank it and Crystal Lake as the two most scenic. The best campsites at the upper lake can be found in the woods along the east shore of the lake, and hopefully out of the wind, which can be horrendous here at times. If it hasn't winterkilled, Upper Powderhorn Lake can have some fantastic (though moody) cutthroat fishing, with fish commonly eighteen inches or better, and an occasional line-breaker.

Whether you fish or not, though, the Powderhorn Lakes are a bargain for your effort. It costs you a bit physically to reach them, but you'll receive two priceless gems for only slightly more than the cost of one!

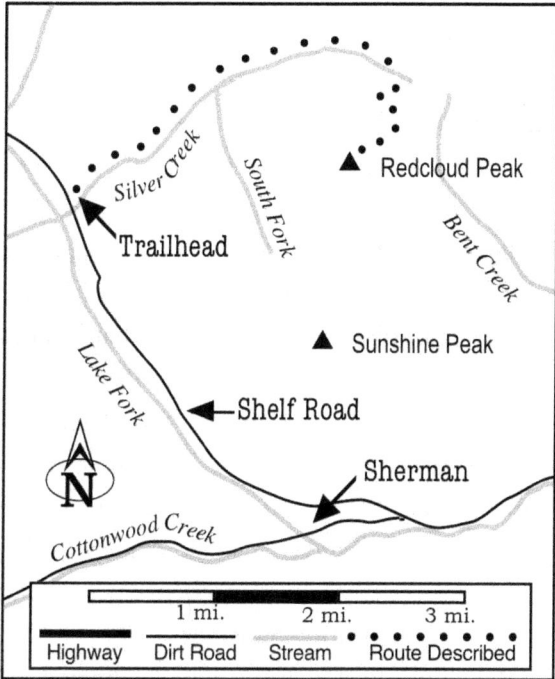

Silver Creek

South Fork

Redcloud Peak

Bent Creek

Trailhead

Sunshine Peak

Lake Fork

Shelf Road

Sherman

Cottonwood Creek

N

	1 mi.	2 mi.	3 mi.
Highway	Dirt Road	Stream • • •	Route Described

10 Redcloud Peak

High mountain summits in the San Juans are not created equal. Although many are of comparable height, in form they divide into two varieties. The first I would call true peaks: they rise to sharp points and scratch a dramatic outline against the Colorado sky. Wetterhorn and Uncompahgre Peaks are two mountains in the Lake City area that fit this description. The second category I would call "whalebacks," and by far, most of Colorado's high mountains are of this variety. A whaleback mountain is one with broad, rolling ridges, and one that is more impressive for its overall massiveness than its drama. Fortunately for hikers, whalebacks are usually easily ascended and offer spectacular views. Redcloud Peak, rising to 14,034´ not far southwest of Lake City, is a true whaleback that makes a great day hike by itself or in combination with neighboring Sunshine Peak.

Redcloud Peak's story actually begins far back in geological time with a structural feature now called the Lake City Caldera. The Lake City Caldera was a huge bowl formed by the collapse of an ancient volcano. When the volcano fell in on itself, two significant results occurred. First, like a bowl with water, the caldera filled with molten lava flows, and second, it created a large circular fault around its rim. Today, the courses of the Lake Fork on the south and

Henson Creek on the north clearly trace the route of the fault, and Redcloud Peak rises as the highest remnant of the filled caldera. Its distinctive reddish hue is a result of subsequent weathering of iron oxide as the volcanic rock has eroded.

Though "Redcloud" sounds like a name that could well belong to an Indian chief, the peak's name was actually the creation of J. C. Spiller in 1874. In that year, two independent government surveys were engaged in a friendly competition in mapping the largely unexplored Colorado Rockies. Dr. Ferdinand V. Hayden headed up the United States Geological and Geographical Survey of the Territories, and Lieutenant George M. Wheeler commanded the United States Geographical Survey West of the Hundredth Meridian. In time, they became known simply as the Hayden Survey and the Wheeler Survey. Both surveys were instrumental in clarifying the geography of the Territory of Colorado, and their members often made the first recorded ascents of many of its highest peaks.

Both surveys were extremely active in the San Juans in the summer of 1874, a full year before Lake City was founded. Hayden's men ascended what they called simply Station 12 (later to be named Sunshine Peak), but apparently did not climb the higher peak (Redcloud) adjoining it to the north.

Topographer J. C. Spiller of the Wheeler Survey, however, was attracted by the cloud like billowy upper ridges of Station 12's neighbor, and he scaled the peak (probably from Burrows Park) and proposed the name "Red Cloud." Interestingly, Redcloud is one of the few Wheeler Survey names that has persisted. Certainly Spiller's description remains extremely apt.

Although Redcloud can be climbed from any point on the compass, the Silver Creek approach is by far the easiest and quickest. This route is a reasonable day hike and includes the option of adding a climb of Sunshine as well.

To reach the trailhead, drive up the Cinnamon Pass Road from Lake City for about twenty miles. This will put you beyond the Shelf Road and into the lower portion of Burrows Park. Just beyond the crossing of Silver Creek, the sign indicating the Silver Creek Trail and Red-cloud Peak will be seen on the right. A short spur road leads to abundant parking space in the roadside meadow.

The Silver Creek Trail is one of those that doesn't dally around gaining elevation. Within ten minutes of leaving the car you'll probably be panting hard as the path climbs steadily through the spruce/fir forest. Feel free to stop as often as you wish though, to enjoy the expanding view across the Lake Fork to Handies Peak and Grizzly Gulch, or just to listen to the cascading stream below the trail The trail climbs steadily for about two miles until it reaches timberline at about 11,600´. A final moderately-steep section then leads you into upper Silver Creek Basin, one of those gorgeous San Juan places that is a fine destination in its own right. At just above 12,000´, the trail moderates for about one half-mile, and in the summer you can enjoy abundant green meadows and blue columbine here. But don't loiter too long—you'll want to arrive at Redcloud's summit before the thunderstorms!

At mile three the trail begins a short switchback assault to the 13,000´ pass on Redcloud's northeast ridge. The pass is a good place for a break and refueling in preparation for the final 1,000´, the steepest of the trip. You'll most likely pause many times on this final section, "enjoying the view," of course.

After 800 vertical feet, the red ridge suddenly moderates, and you'll be on top of the whaleback. It's then only 200´ more climbing and an easy stroll to the rounded summit itself. If the weather is good (as it has never been when I've been on Redcloud's summit), you'll want to admire the view of Wetterhorn and Uncompahgre to the north, the Sneffels Range to the west, and Handies, the Needles, and Rio Grande Pyramid to the south. Sign the summit register and then decide if you want to add the three-mile round trip to Sunshine. Many hikers can do this easily, but if you're already exhausted on top of Redcloud, wisdom may dictate to be satisfied with one Fourteener for the day. When you've had your fill of the view from the summit, you may return via the route you ascended, or take a steep shortcut down a cairn-marked route on Redcloud's northwest ridge. Be cautioned, though, that this is a route and not a trail, and involves plenty of scree. It ultimately takes you into the South Fork of Silver Creek, which then rejoins the ascent trail. Descending this way will save about one mile of hiking, but is best negotiated by those confident walking down sliding masses of small rocks!

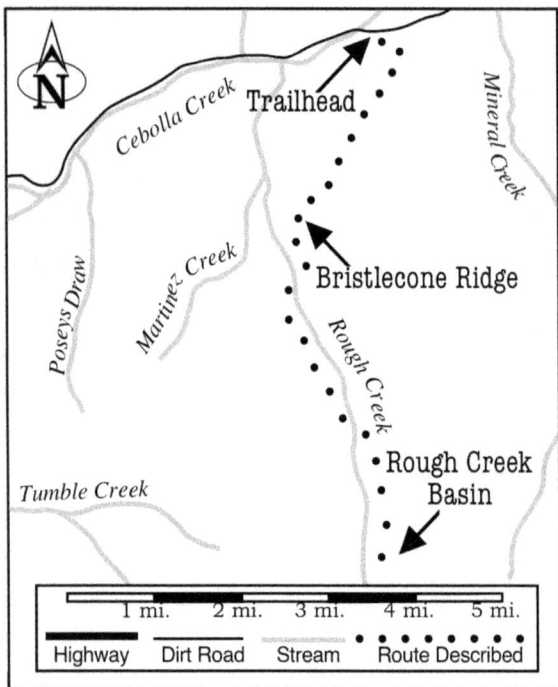

Map labels:
- N (compass)
- Cebolla Creek
- Trailhead
- Mineral Creek
- Poseys Draw
- Martinez Creek
- Bristlecone Ridge
- Rough Creek
- Tumble Creek
- Rough Creek Basin

Scale: 1 mi. 2 mi. 3 mi. 4 mi. 5 mi.

Legend: Highway | Dirt Road | Stream | Route Described

11 Rough Creek

Not long ago I was asked by a young couple for a suggestion of a short scenic backpacking hike that would not be overrun with people. It was a tall order, since most easily accessible trails are heavily travelled, especially during the Fourth of July week when this inquiry occurred. Once the maps were unfolded, however, it didn't take long to settle on a recommendation of Rough Creek, an unspoiled tributary to Cebolla Creek that sees many times more elk than hikers tread its trail. Those looking for a relatively moderate hike into the solitude of wilderness would do well to consider a venture up Rough Creek when the crowds get to be a bit too much.

To reach the Rough Creek trailhead, drive from Lake City up Slumgullion Pass for about nine miles to County Road 50, the Cathedral/Powderhorn road. Take this good gravel road for approximately eleven miles to the signed Rough Creek trailhead. Odds are, unless you're here during hunting season, yours will be the only vehicle at the trailhead—a real rarity in the San Juans during the summer! From here on, you'll be within the La Garita Wilderness Area, so travel is limited to foot or horseback.

After signing in at the trailhead register, follow the trail as it climbs gradually to the south. Until the trail reaches Rough Creek itself, three miles and 1,000 vertical feet further, it passes no water, so be sure to have plenty with you for this section of the trail.

The Rough Creek Trail climbs steadily (but never very steeply) through the highlands separating Pasture and Rough Creeks. Here the land is quite dry, and numerous grassy and rocky parks are separated by stands of ponderosa pine, Douglas Fir, Englemann spruce and a few bristlecone pine. In small hollows the vegetation grows a bit more lushly, and you may spot wild irises, geraniums, and strawberries, the latter which should provide a snack or two later in the summer. If you hike this portion in May, look and listen for elk that frequent these foothills during the winter and spring months.

The trail climbs gradually but steadily, and within a couple of miles you will probably be surprised to see how much elevation you have actually gained. Looking north, the trailhead is lost in the canyon of Cebolla Creek, now far below the broad-shouldered mass of Calf Creek Plateau. Best of all, perhaps, nothing man-made but the narrow Rough Creek Trail itself can be seen for miles in any direction.

At a point about two and one-half miles up the trail, you will crest a ridge and be able to hear the rushing of Rough Creek several hundred feet below. If you're hot and dry at this point, it will certainly be a very comforting sound! Across the valley to the west, several parks that blanket the hillside are great places to scan in the morning or evening hours for deer or elk.

The trail contours along the Rough Creek gorge for a half-mile or so, and in the process passes through one of the more interesting stands of bristlecone pine I have visited. Bristlecones are usually a twisted and gnarled species, bent and sculpted by harsh climate. Here, however, the bristlecones grow unusually straight and tall, perhaps a result of kinder winds here than elsewhere. Whatever the exact causes, the grove is an interesting example of bristlecones not behaving like bristlecones!

A short distance beyond "Bristlecone Ridge," a number of important changes converge. First, the trail finally comes within sight of Rough Creek, a tumbling, wild Colorado mountain stream at its best Second, the vegetation zone changes from the montane to the subalpine zone, and from here upstream, quaking aspen and Englemann spruce blanket the mountainsides rather densely. Look for a change in flower species as well—red columbine, violets, and jacobs ladder will become much more abundant as daisies and irises decrease. Third, the Rough Creek trail intersects the Cebolla Trail, a little-used sheep driveway that traverses much of the northern flank of the La Garitas.

The Rough Creek Trail crosses the stream on the remains of a stock driveway bridge, and a small campsite or two can be found near the stream. Better sites, but not as close to the water, can also be found a short distance upstream in some lovely open stands of aspen. This area, about three miles from the trailhead, would be an excellent base camp for an extended stay, as day hikes could be made from here to the high country at the head of Rough Creek, and both directions up the Cebolla Trail toward Martinez Creek or Mineral Park, all of which give a taste of wilderness at its finest.

While the Cebolla Trail junction is a good destination for a backpack or a day hike, if you have the time it is definitely worthwhile to continue up the Rough Creek trail to the basin at its head. Not far south of the junction, beavers are doing a masterful job of damming the flow of Rough Creek, and you could easily spend a day marvelling at their logging and engineering practices. Evening is probably the best time to look for the animals themselves at work. Despite the beavers' efforts, however, trout do not live in any of the ponds—a fact that may explain why Rough Creek is seldom visited. Rough Creek from its confluence with Martinez Creek on down does support trout, though, and fishermen looking for a pristine experience on a small stream can find no better than lower Rough Creek. However, there is no trail in lower Rough Creek and navigating in places can indeed be rough!

Above the Cebolla Trail junction, the Rough Creek Trail winds for nearly a mile through a large stand of aspen and then begins to climb out of the beaver dam valley and into rockier terrain. The hillside you'll be climbing is probably a moraine left behind by the glacier that carved the upper cirque of the Rough Creek valley. Here the trail crosses an occasional spring, and in the early part of the season, portions of it may be muddy. The trail is steeper here, but you'll be rewarded with fine views of an impressive eroded rock formation on the opposite mountainside, many varieties of flowers and perhaps some wildlife. The last time I was here, I played leapfrog with a healthy young elk determined to elude me in this narrow valley.

At about 11,000 feet and five miles from the trailhead, the path levels once again and you'll suddenly behold the full glory of upper Rough Creek basin. Here is a classic high country basin, complete with expansive meadows, a winding stream, and black timber rising to meet unnamed peaks on three sides. It is a place you could easily spend a day, a week or even a summer drinking in its beauty. Unfortunately, a day hike will not permit you to spend much time here, so a backpack including this basin as a destination would be ideal. The Rough Creek trail meets the Skyline Trail at the head of the basin, permitting longer trips and access to even more wild and beautiful country.

Rough Creek is not one of those places you'll see pictured on Colorado calendars, but some places of exceptional beauty and solitude escape the calendar photographer's lens. Rough Creek is just one such place, and if you don't mind a few miles of lonely trail in the wilderness, "roughing it" up Rough Creek may become one of the more pleasant experiences of your summer in the San Juans.

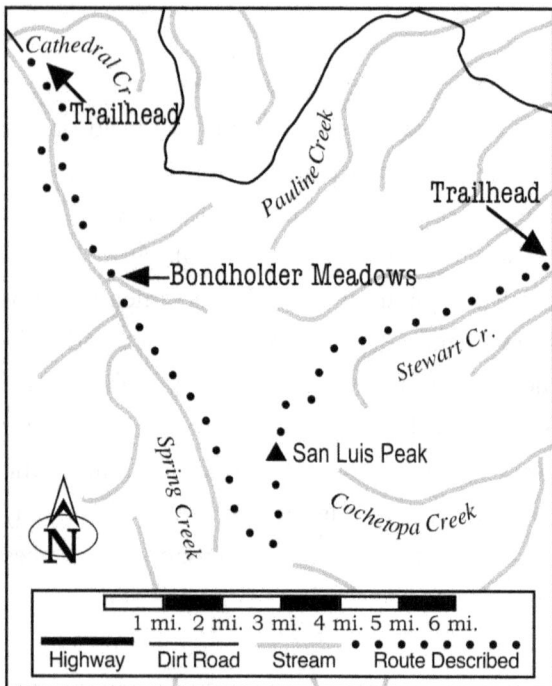

Map showing trailheads, Cathedral Cr., Pauline Creek, Bondholder Meadows, Stewart Cr., San Luis Peak, Spring Creek, and Cocheropa Creek.

1 mi. 2 mi. 3 mi. 4 mi. 5 mi. 6 mi.			
Highway	Dirt Road	Stream	Route Described

12 San Luis Peak

Wilderness peaks are hard to come by these days, especially among Colorado mountains that rise over 14,000 feet above the sea. It seems that many outdoor lovers, presumably in search of the solitude of high mountains, have achieved the ultimate irony by stumbling over themselves in order to find it. Uncompahgre Peak, for example, is generally not a good peak on which to get away from people on any given day during July or August. Happily, though, a few blue-blooded wilderness mountains remain, and San Luis Peak, southeast of Lake City, endures as a fine specimen of this vanishing breed.

Isolation keeps 14,014´ San Luis Peak relatively quiet while dozens of other peaks are overrun weekend after weekend. San Luis rises far from any major population centers (unless you consider Creede a major population center) and most climbs of this mountain require a very long day hike or even an overnight backpack. As a result, San Luis is enjoyed primarily by climbers who appreciate the value of high country wilderness and don't mind in the least pushing tired legs up a few extra miles of rocky trail in order to find it.

San Luis Peak is the highest point of the La Garita Mountain Range and rises twenty miles east of Lake City. As Colorado mountains go,

San Luis is not especially spectacular, just a long rolling ridge of volcanic rock projecting north from the Continental Divide. In addition, San Luis is invisible from many vantage points, often hidden by its northern neighbor Stewart Peak, far and away the most prominent peak in the La Garitas. As a result, San Luis' history is somewhat obscure, while that of Stewart is well-documented.

Although who named San Luis is lost to history, it is clear for whom the mountain was named. King Louis IX of France was one of the most popular monarchs of the thirteenth century, and his pietism and efforts in the Crusades led to his canonization after his death. "San Luis" is the Spanish form of Saint Louis, and language-conscious climbers should call it "San Looeese" instead of "San Looie," which is a strange mix of Spanish and French.

Historian John Jerome Hart suggests that San Luis Peak probably acquired its name from the nearby San Luis Valley, which in turn was named by an unknown Spanish explorer who hailed from a town whose patron saint was

Saint Louis. This is quite plausible, since even today many Latin American communities are named San Luis, or incorporate San Luis into a longer name.

The mountaineer who first reached San Luis' summit is as anonymous as its name giver. For many years it was assumed that Franklin Rhoda of the Hayden Survey climbed the peak in 1874 for triangulation purposes, but this theory has recently been challenged by writer Mike Foster who asserts that Rhoda climbed a 13,502´ peak to the west of San Luis instead. Foster is probably correct, and there is an equal probability that San Luis, by no means a difficult climb, was first ascended by an unknown Ute, fur trapper, or prospector.

As is the case with most mountains over the years, San Luis' elevation has changed. Improved surveying technology rather than mountain-moving forces is the cause, and since the 1950s, San Luis has "shrunk, from 14,149´ to 14,014´. Nearby Stewart Peak has "lost" less actual footage, but has dropped out of the Fourteener club from 14,060´ to 13,983´. Oddly enough, then, the once well-known Stewart is now the more obscure of the two, since it is currently "merely" a Thirteener!

With the exception of a small locale near Creede, the La Garitas are not highly mineralized, and thus San Luis is without the prospectors' pock marking that scars much of the San Juans. The lack of man's intrusion was a major factor in the designation of the La Garita Wilderness Area that fully surrounds the peak.

San Luis is an excellent climb for hikers in good physical condition. Some of the approach trails are rather long and are best combined with an overnight backpack. On all trail approaches climbers should remember that they are in a Wilderness Area and should tread and camp lightly.

The nearest approach to San Luis from Lake City is via Cathedral. From Cathedral (fifteen miles down the Cebolla Road from Slumgullion Pass) drive to the Cadwell Ranch up Spring Creek. Along the road you will have a rare glimpse of San Luis looming up on the east side of the valley. At road's end, you will need to ask permission to hike across private property for a couple of miles on your way to Bondholder Meadows, six miles distant and a good place for a base camp. The entire Spring Creek valley is mountain beauty at its finest and is a place you'll long remember whether you climb the mountain or not.

From Bondholder Meadows, the trail continues about five more miles to reach the Continental Divide and then east to cross San Luis' easy south ridge. Once on top, you'll have a great view of not only the entire La Garita Mountain Range, but also the Elk Mountains, Sawatch Range, and a good portion of the heart of the San Juans.

The shortest hike (but longest drive) to San Luis is via the Stewart Creek Trail, which is about three hours from Lake City over rough dirt roads via Los Piños Pass and the Big Meadows Road. Check your maps carefully to avoid getting lost on the roads! The Stewart Creek route follows a trail most of the distance to the summit, but even though it is the shortest route on San Luis, plan on a round trip of twelve miles! Other approaches to San Luis are possible (including one from Creede), but as I review all these route options, I am thoroughly convinced that an extended backpacking or horsepacking trip is the best way to enjoy San Luis and its surrounding valleys. A day trip from any approach simply does not do the mountain justice, In most years, access roads and trails will be open from the middle of June until October. Local inquiry can provide specific road and trail information.

As more and more Colorado peaks feel the press of civilization, San Luis persists as a mountain of the wilderness. It is a peak you enjoy not so much for the sake of the mountain alone as for the wild country it oversees. Here you will more likely meet a bighorn ram on the trail than another human being, and you will count many times more columbine blossoms than candy wrappers. You will remember again how milky the Milky Way really is and you will find yourself redefining "quiet". Sip teeth-numbing water from a spring, sing with a choir of whistling marmots, nestle into a green alpine carpet, and feel the wilderness—for San Luis Peak has the wilderness in its soul.

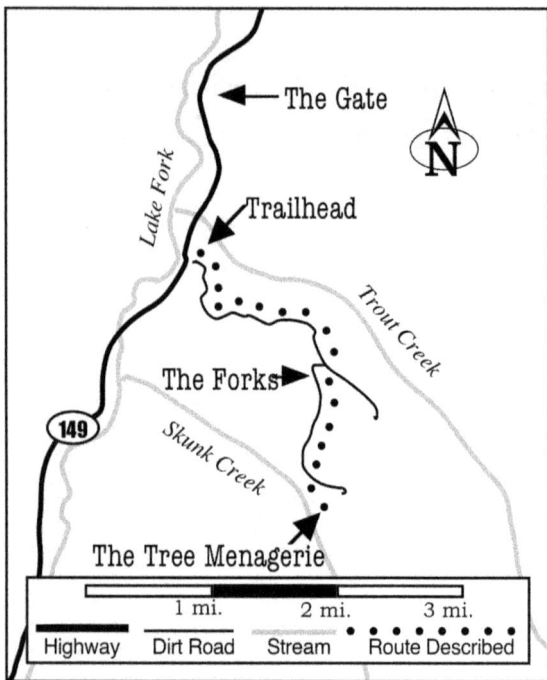

The Gate

Trailhead

Lake Fork

Trout Creek

The Forks

149

Skunk Creek

The Tree Menagerie

1 mi.	2 mi.	3 mi.
Highway	Dirt Road	Stream	Route Described

13 Skunk Creek Road

The Hidden Country. That's my name for a swath of land nearly twenty miles in length on the east side of the Lake Fork River north of Lake City. Bounded on the west by the river and on the east by the crest of Cannibal and

Calf Creek Plateaus, it is a chunk of land that is seldom travelled by visitors to Lake City, and not without good reason. Most of the access routes into the Hidden Country are privately controlled, and those that aren't involve long and arduous treks over the plateaus to the east, journeys that very few are willing to undertake. As a result, the Hidden Country is sixty square miles of Rocky Mountain backcountry tantalizingly close but with little public access.

The Skunk Creek Road, or actually the Skunk Creek Road system, provides an excellent introduction to the diversity and beauty of the Hidden Country, easily accessible to the hiker or off-road vehicle. The relatively low elevation of the Skunk Creek area (8,000 to 9,000 feet) makes it a great choice for April or May hiking or jeeping when the high country is still snowed in. No matter when you choose to visit this section of BLM land, you will likely have it all to yourself, except during hunting season when deer and elk hunters visit the area.

The Skunk Creek Road is easily reached from Lake City, but since it is not prominently signed, you'll need to keep a close eye out for the turnoff and gate. From Lake City, drive approximately fifteen miles north on 149 to a point only .7 miles north of the highway bridge. Here, almost directly across the road from a fishermen's parking area, look for a dirt track entering the highway from the east (right). Currently, the BLM has a small sign indicating Road 3018, but it is not easily seen from the highway.

The Skunk Creek Road can be travelled by jeep, of course, but you'll miss much that it has to offer. It is better seen on foot, horseback, or possibly even mountain bike (but be prepared for a couple of pedal-straining hills!).

Skunk Creek is a name a bit misleading for this road, since Skunk Creek lies only near its end. The road begins by following a smaller unnamed intermittent drainage that I call Juniper Creek. Not surprisingly, you'll notice a large number of Rocky Mountain junipers growing in this drainage—in fact, some of the largest junipers I have seen in the Lake Fork Valley. They are wonderful, twisted, weather defying plants, and many of them I imagine being depicted on a Chinese landscape painting. The smaller junipers look like green pyramids looming from a sea of sagebrush, and some of these are "nurse trees" for young Douglas Firs, which are less sun-tolerant. In time, the firs will greatly outsize their "nurses," and the junipers will die out.

The road climbs steeply for the first eighth mile or so, but then moderates a bit in an upland of sage, juniper, and ponderosa pine. You will probably see birds in this area, including flickers, juncos, chickadees, ravens, hawks, and the mascot of Juniper Creek, the Townsend's Solitaire. While humans find juniper berries practically inedible (try one if you don't believe me!) Townsend's Solitaires love them and will be found year-round in places such as Juniper Creek.

Before long, the road drops back down toward Juniper Creek and crosses a couple of dry tributaries coming in from the south. All of the Juniper Creek tributaries are hikable, and some have jeep roads. If you have the time, it can be enjoyable to explore several of them—a goal not unrealistic since these branches are less than a mile in length.

At about a mile and a half from the highway, the road turns sharply south and soon you'll be at "The Forks," a place where three main branches of Juniper Creek divide. Again, all of the branches can be explored, but the main road follows the middle fork, heading directly for a surprising grove of aspen in these sage-and-pine dominated hills.

The aspen grove is a pleasant oasis of shade on a warm summer's afternoon, and holds some secrets for those who look around. The battle-scarred trunks bear the signs of many winters of elk browsing and a bit of human activity as well. Although carving up tree trunks with human initials is now rightfully considered a deplorable practice, some inscriptions are old enough to have historical value. One of the these trees in this grove has the barely discernible "1924" etched on it, and just above that, "1919"—two of the oldest examples of aspen graffiti I have seen. This too, obviously indicates the age of the trees, which must have been aged at the time of the inscriptions. Who made them and why they were in this obscure aspen grove in a nameless drainage remains lost to history.

The road continues climbing steadily beyond the aspen grove, and the presence of more aspen further up signals a reliable source of moisture. Before long, the source becomes apparent in the form of a cold spring issuing from the hillside to the left of the road. The spring feeds a small pond, which is of interest with its aquatic plants, water striders and salamanders, all of which seem a bit out of place here.

A few hundred yards above the pond, the road crests a divide and splits once again. The left hand fork proceeds steeply up the valley, but the right hand fork drops gently over the ridge and into Skunk Creek proper. This fork contours through a pleasant grove of ponderosa pine and Douglas fir, and when it reaches Skunk Creek (a small permanent stream), you will be in a real botanical menagerie. At one point, several trees can be found growing within fifty feet of one another that normally aren't close neighbors. Look around and you'll discover Ponderosa pine, Douglas fir, Rocky Mountain juniper, aspen, Colorado blue spruce, and what I believe are a few fine specimens of white fir, which are relatively scarce in these parts.

The "tree menagerie" on Skunk Creek is a good destination for a spring day hike here, for although a jeep road of sorts continues a ways up the creek, it will be snowed in until later in the summer. Given the relatively gentle terrain and seven parallel tributaries of Juniper Creek, you'll have many choices for returning to the trailhead by a route other than the one described. Doing this, most day hikes will wind up gaining about 1,000′ in elevation and will be four or five miles round-trip. If you leave the roads, though, it helps to have a topographic map.

Many other surprises await the explorer in the Skunk Creek vicinity. The ancient remains of a cabin, a pond deep enough for swimming, and much more I don't know about hides in this wild corner of the Lake Fork Valley. Discover a bit of the Hidden Country for yourself, and if there's a trace of explorer in you at all, you'll be back for more.

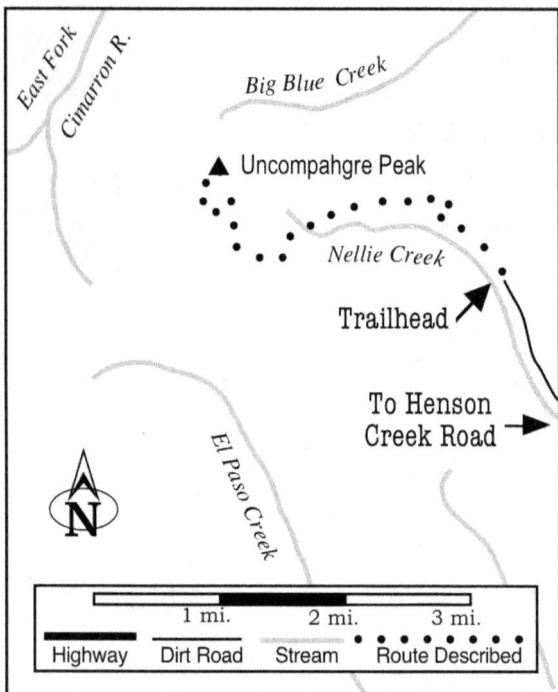

Map showing Uncompahgre Peak area with East Fork Cimarron R., Big Blue Creek, Nellie Creek, El Paso Creek, Trailhead, and route "To Henson Creek Road."

Legend:
- Highway
- Dirt Road
- Stream
- Route Described

Scale: 1 mi., 2 mi., 3 mi.

14 Uncompahgre Peak

From the summit of Colorado's highest peak, Mount Elbert, the rest of the state falls away like a giant relief map. On a clear day the observant mountaineer can easily distinguish many of the state's other great peaks—Massive,

Holy Cross, Pikes, and Harvard, but the distant San Juans remain largely a featureless uplifted mass on the distant horizon. Featureless, that is, with the single exception of the unmistakable bulk of Uncompahgre Peak, the highest point in the San Juans. Indeed, the impressive summit block of Uncompahgre is unique in form among Colorado mountains, and makes it a more distinguishable landmark from a distance than Mount Elbert itself. It is fitting that this peak is the capstone of the largest mountain range in the state.

Uncompahgre Peak rises to 14,309 feet, falling only 125 feet short of being the highest peak in the Rockies, and less than 200 feet short of Mount Whitney, the highest peak in the contiguous United States. Only five other Colorado mountains reach higher. Fortunately, Uncompahgre is not a difficult climb, and each year hundreds of people of all ages thrill to the highest view in the San Juans.

As prominent as it is, Uncompahgre has been a landmark for generations. Its name is Ute, and is probably derived from a phrase meaning "hot water spring." The hot springs in question are those near the present town of Ouray, and the name was then applied to the Uncompahgre River, and ultimately to the great peak that looms near the river's source. Since few Ute names have survived in the San Juans, it is appropriate that this one remains on the great peak. Other names have from time to time been proposed for the mountain, including "The Leaning Tower," "Capitol Mountain," and "Mount Chauvenet," the latter for a nineteenth century professor of astronomy. Uncompahgre has held off all of these challenges, though, and proudly remains "Unc" to those who know it best.

Uncompahgre was certainly climbed by Indians, and probably prospectors in the late 1860s or early 1870s, but the first recorded ascent was in the summer of 1874 by A. D. Wilson and Franklin Rhoda of the Hayden Survey, who made the first recorded climbs of many of the peaks in the San Juans. Wilson and Rhoda found, however, that they shared the peak with a grizzly bear, not an unusual occurrence in those days. Rhoda later bemoaned the lack of true solitude in the mountains even in those early days: "When you feel like you are treading a path never before trod by a living being … if some such vile, worldly thing such as a paper collar or a whisky bottle does not intrude itself on the site, some beastly quadruped must …" Today, given the human crowds in many parts of the San Juans, Rhoda would probably welcome the sight of a grizzly bear!

As imposing as it appears, Uncompahgre Peak is nevertheless one of the two easiest Fourteeners in the Lake City area to scale (the other being Handies from American Basin). An excellent trail reaches Uncompahgre's summit from Nellie Creek, and acclimated folks pushing eighty years have been known to make it to the summit, as well as children not a tenth that old. Given proper acclimation, good weather and common climbing sense, this summit is well within the abilities of nearly anyone who can hike six or seven miles in a day.

The Uncompahgre Peak Trail begins at the end of the Nellie Creek Road, four miles above its junction with the Henson Creek Road. Four-wheel drive is best for the Nellie Creek road, but some high center two-wheel drives may be able to make it as well.

The trail begins near 11,400 feet, in the heart of the tall spruce and fir of the subalpine zone. The headwaters of Nellie Creek splash nearby, and pine grosbeaks and Clark's nutcrackers may be spotted. Within a mile of moderate climbing the trail breaks out of the trees and into the magical world above timberline. Here you'll have a magnificent unobstructed view of the peak and a great locale in which to take photos of your companions heading up the trail.

At about two miles, a fork is reached, with the left hand one heading downhill into the El Paso Creek drainage. Please take note of this junction, for on the descent, more than once Hinsdale County Search and Rescue has been activated to locate a party which mistakenly turned off into El Paso Creek instead of returning to their vehicle at Nellie Creek. From the junction, it is 1,100 feet vertical and about a mile to the summit, with only one short steep section through some talus at about 14,000 feet. The summit is surprisingly flat, and had Uncompahgre kept going up instead of flattening out, it would be an easy winner for the highest peak in the state!

The view from Uncompahgre is, of course, magnificent. Most of western Colorado and some of eastern Utah is visible: the La Sal Mountains, Grand Mesa, the West Elk and Elk Ranges near Aspen, the Sawatch Range (including Mount Elbert), the Sangre de Cristos, and, of course, nearly all of the San Juans. There is also a view straight down from Uncompahgre, 1,000 feet off of the north face. Those who have a fear of long drops will want to stay well back from the edge! Please avoid the urge to toss rocks off of this precipice (you never know who may be far below).

One final word: if the day is clear and glorious, take your time to lounge on Uncompahgre's summit, but if it is threatening at all, get down in a hurry. I don't know about you, but in a lightning storm I sure wouldn't want to be the highest lightning rod in the San Juans!

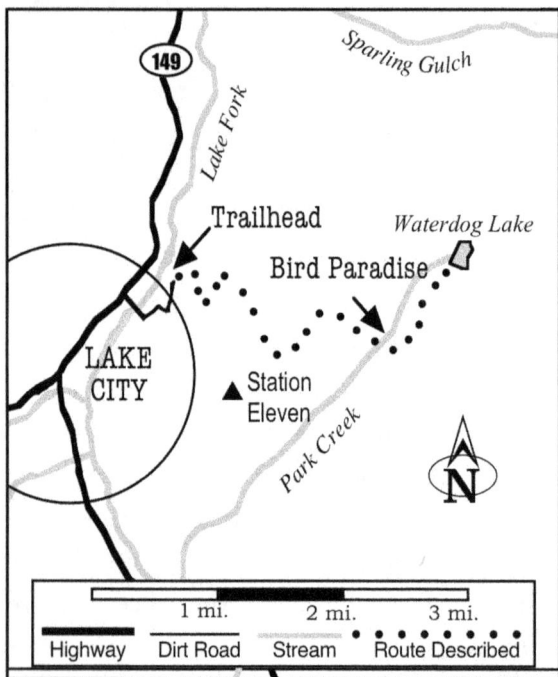

On the map: 149, Sparling Gulch, Lake Fork, Trailhead, Waterdog Lake, Bird Paradise, LAKE CITY, Station Eleven, Park Creek, N

| 1 mi. | 2 mi. | 3 mi. |
| Highway | Dirt Road | Stream | Route Described |

15 Waterdog Lake

Lake City is surrounded on three sides by a mountain balcony. Lake City's balcony is supported by pillars of bedrock, flanked with rolling meadows and stained with the green of spruce and the white of aspen. Here, from two to three thousand feet above town, Lake City is ringed by the "second-floor" attractions of Crystal Lake, Larson Lakes, Round Top Mountain, Station Eleven and Waterdog Lake. Those who take the time to leave Lake City's "ground floor" and ascend the rocky steps to the balcony will discover some wonderful country well worth the steep hiking required to get there.

Waterdog Lake is an excellent destination for those interested in sampling the balcony country. Though the lake lies only two miles from town as the crow flies, the trail stretches this to twice the distance while climbing 2,500 feet. With an early start and proper acclimation, a hike to Waterdog Lake can be a relatively leisurely one-day trip with ample time for a bit of relaxing or angling at the lake. Be prepared, though, for some steep hiking at the outset.

The Waterdog Lake Trail begins rather unceremoniously at Lake City's sewage treatment plant. Parking is available near the entrance to the plant, at the trailhead sign. Hike the broad trail (actually a road) past the fenced ponds and up the hill to the north. Once the road begins to level out within one tenth mile, watch for the Waterdog Lake sign and trail diverting and climbing the hillside to the right. The trail leaves the road just before the private residence at the top of the hill.

The first part of the Waterdog Lake Trail climbs moderately steeply up the mountainside through an open Douglas fir forest, interspersed with a talus slope or two. The steepness of the trail is partially compensated for by superb views of Lake City and an ever expanding vista of the country across the valley. You can also divert your attention from your gasping lungs by watching for wildflowers that prefer these dry slopes, such as the dry land daisy and the ground-hugging creeping hollygrape. Keeping an eye in the tree crowns, you'll likely spot a Steller's jay or two and perhaps a few mountain chickadees.

After about one-half mile, the trail moderates and crosses under some power lines, but soon it climbs steeply once again, this time up a more densely forested slope. When the trail turns to follow a broad ridge at about 9,800 feet, you'll be in an extensive stand of aspen, and the sights and sounds of Lake City have been left far below. Here the scenery changes from spectacular to intimate. These are quiet woods. A spring-fed pipe trickles into a trough. Red columbines nod in the filtered sun and heart-leaved arnica dot the forest floor. Breeze-caressed trees speak to one another in hushed tones. Don't hurry here.

At about two miles from Lake City, the trail breaks out of the woods and into the surprising expanse of green called Horse Park. Not visible from the valley below, Horse Park is part of Vickers' upper ranch, and must be one of the prettiest places on the balcony. Crossing the meadow, the trail soon intersects a jeep road climbing up from Vickers Ranch. If you lose the trail in the meadow, angle uphill through the meadow and you'll eventually reach the jeep road. The steepest portion of your trip is now past; you can leisurely stroll along the jeep trail the remaining distance to Waterdog Lake. Please hike only on the road, however, since you are crossing private land.

As the road climbs to the upper portion of Horse Park, you'll have a fine view of cone-shaped Station Eleven behind you. Station Eleven was so named in 1874 by the United States government's Hayden Survey. While mapping uncharted regions such as the San Juans, the Hayden Survey established various mountain peaks as triangulation stations for their work. Unlike most San Juan stations that received new names in later years, Station Eleven has retained its title for well over a century.

Near the upper end of Horse Park, the jeep road crosses tiny Park Creek in an area I informally call "Bird Paradise." Lying near the boundaries of the montane and subalpine life zones, and being a mixture of woods, meadows and riparian habitat, this area attracts an unusual variety of birds. If you're fond of looking up species in your field guide, you might just tarry too long here and not make Waterdog Lake!

After crossing Park Creek, the road climbs moderately once again. Here Mesa Seco dominates the eastern skyline. Shortly the meadows and aspen groves give way to a dark forest of Englemann spruce, and if it's a hot day you'll be thankful for the shade. Just beyond the National Forest boundary, the trail climbs a bit more steeply and then Waterdog Lake suddenly shimmers before you.

I have yet to see a mountain lake that I could term anything but beautiful, and Waterdog Lake is no exception. The forest grows right to the water's edge on the approach side, and the opposite shore is bordered by a steep bank of rocks and grass. The seven-acre lake is not too difficult to hike around, and some great sites for a "lazy attack" are found on the opposite shore. As you hike its perimeter, look for the lake's namesakes in shallow water—waterdog is the common name for the immature aquatic form of the tiger salamander.

If you hit it right, Waterdog Lake can provide some excellent fishing. Waterdog Lake used to be populated 100% by brook trout, but in recent years, the lake has been stocked with native Colorado River cutthroat trout. The lake seldom winterkills, and is often one of the earliest high country lakes to open up. If the fish are coming to the top, a fly and bubble combination can do well, but if not, a spinner or bait is the best bet.

Waterdog Lake is one of those places you won't want to hurry from. If you can spend the night, do so—that will allow more time for its character to soak into your soul. But if you can't, at least put down your pack, kick off your boots and soak your tired feet in its cool water. Cast a line for a trout or two, have a picnic or just relax and inhale air so clean it almost squeaks. Whatever you do, I'm sure you'll come away thankful for Waterdog Lake's many gifts—after all, it's not everybody who has such treasures as close as their own balcony!

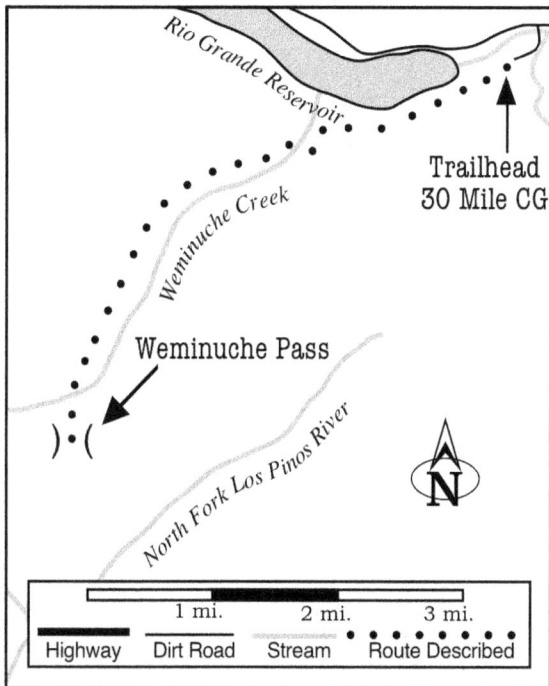

Rio Grande Reservoir

Weminuche Creek

Trailhead
30 Mile CG

Weminuche Pass

North Fork Los Pinos River

N

1 mi.	2 mi.	3 mi.
Highway	Dirt Road	Stream	Route Described

16 Weminuche Pass

One of the lowest crossings of the Continental Divide in the state of Colorado has never heard the roar of jeep or Winnebago. While each week during the summer thousands of motorized vehicles of every kind roll across the divide at higher passes like Monarch, Wolf Creek, and Independence, Weminuche Pass in the heart of the Weminuche Wilderness south of Lake City remains undisturbed except for the quiet plod of hiker's feet or the occasional whinny of a horse. It has been that way for generations at this gap in the San Juans, and those who travel there today touch lives in a small way with the Indians, fur trappers and backcountry adventurers who have passed through this wilderness gateway before them, for Weminuche Pass is uniquely laden with both history and wilderness.

Weminuche Pass, at approximately 10,500´ (its precise elevation has not been recorded on maps), is the lowest crossing of the Continental Divide in Hinsdale County. By air it lies about twenty-four miles almost due south of Lake City, but by road and trail most of us need to travel about twice that distance to reach this remote place. Thirty Mile Campground just below Rio Grande Reservoir is the jumping off point for the pass and a good portion of the vast Weminuche Wilderness.

Weminuche Pass has been well known to humans for centuries. The earliest white visitors to the San Juans found well-travelled paths over the pass that had been used by the Weminuche band of Ute Indians, and probably other Indians before them. The pass is a natural passageway between the Rio Grande drainage to the north and the long Los Piños drainage to the south. Indians looking for game during the summer knew a good shortcut when they saw one, and Weminuche Pass served them well. Undoubtedly many hunts were successful at the pass itself, since its meadows were also a natural corridor for big game.

The first European to venture across Weminuche Pass is not known, but it is possible that it was some unknown Spanish explorer or missionary from the frontier outpost of Santa Fe in the seventeenth or eighteenth centuries. The Rio Grande valley was a natural highway into much of southern Colorado, and Spanish adventurers exploring the Rio Grande near its source could have easily ventured five more miles up well-worn Indian paths to its crest.

Unfortunately, most of the Spaniards explored much but wrote little, leaving the identity of the first European visitor to Weminuche Pass a mystery.

The first white man who produced any evidence that he visited Weminuche Pass was mountain man James Pattie in 1827. Directed by Ute Indians up the Los Piños River from the south, Pattie supposedly made his trip to Weminuche Pass in May and found snow drifts higher than a man on a horse—not an unlikely possibility. Whether Pattie's story was true or not, though (mountain men have been known to exaggerate), since fur trappers were apt to explore nearly every Colorado valley for beaver, Pattie or some other contemporary fur trapper certainly made his way up the pass from one side or the other.

Had geography placed Weminuche Pass almost anywhere else in the state, it certainly would have become a route for one of the many narrow gauge railroads that breached the Continental Divide during the 1870s and 1880s. The Colorado Rockies were an imposing barrier to the railroad builders and they competed vigorously for the easiest routes through. Weminuche Pass, though, oriented from north to south from one remote drainage to another remote drainage, was not nearly as attractive as those passes that offered access from east to west or into nearby booming mining camps. As a result, Weminuche Pass remained a hiking and horseback route, much to the delight of seekers of wilderness.

Those who seek to explore this pass today will find the shortest route beginning at Thirtymile Campground on the Rio Grande Reservoir Road. The pass is only five miles and 1,300 feet of elevation gain by good trail, and thus is accessible on a day hike, but those who wish to absorb the full beauty of the place should plan on a backpack or horsepack trip. Weminuche Pass allows access into too much country to make short trips very satisfying.

Beginning from Thirtymile Campground, the hiker will find it taking a while to get a true "wilderness feeling." For a half-mile or so the trail is paralleled by a phone line, and then it passes by Rio Grande Reservoir, somewhat scenic when full, but much less than scenic when it is not. Automobile traffic may be seen and heard from across the reservoir for over a mile, but when the trail finally begins to climb steadily and then turns south up Weminuche Creek, things begin to change for the better. In these predominately aspen woods, blue columbine bloom with profusion, a rarity at this relatively low elevation. Soon the sound of the creek drowns out any distant noise, and a crossing of the creek on a rustic bridge at mile two is an excellent site for a break. The whitewater cascades here will soon make you forget the sights and sounds of civilization and help you anticipate the wilderness ahead.

After a short steep climb above the bridge, the trail moderates in the meadowed upper valley of Weminuche Creek. The willows along the creek are a good place to look for elk, and the creek is good fishing for brook trout. Those prepared to camp may want to choose a site along this part of the trail, though campsites in the trees here will be a ways above water.

A good-sized stream and excellent campsite is reached at mile 4.75, and a short distance later, you'll reach Weminuche Pass itself, though it is not signed. In fact, the pass is so flat you'll have to look carefully in the broad meadow below you to discern which way the water is flowing. The only man made intrusion here is the Raber Lohr Ditch, built in 1935 to take water from the Pacific side to the Atlantic. Otherwise, the pass is much as it appeared to the Utes and James Pattie—a long broad meadow two miles long and nearly a mile wide, lined on both sides with steep ramparts of forest and rock. Through the meadow winds the headwaters of the Los Piños River, which can produce a gorgeous cutthroat trout or two for the cautious fisherman.

Tarry at Weminuche Pass for an hour or a week—it is like nowhere else in the San Juans. Let your imagination take you back to the Indians and explorers who have admired this place before. They too, I think, would be pleased that at least this pass remains a wilderness domain of man without machine.

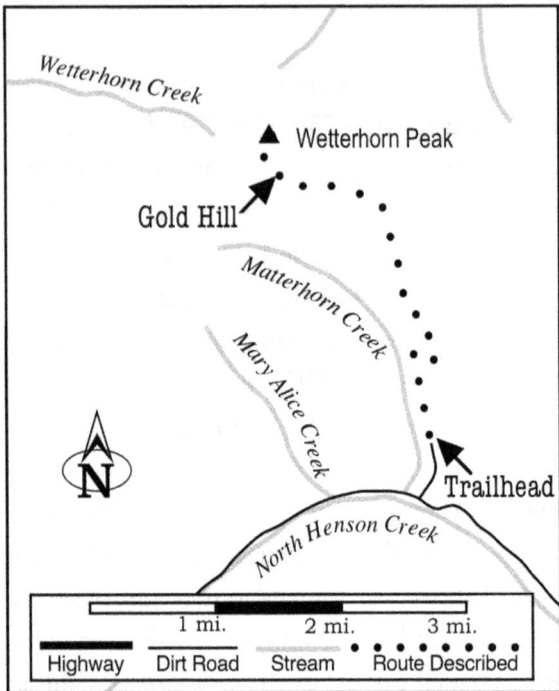

Map labels: Wetterhorn Creek, Wetterhorn Peak, Gold Hill, Matterhorn Creek, Mary Alice Creek, North Henson Creek, Trailhead, N

Scale: 1 mi. — 2 mi. — 3 mi.

Legend: Highway | Dirt Road | Stream | Route Described

17 Wetterhorn Peak

One of the most dramatic and best-loved views in the Lake City area is that from Windy Point on Slumgullion Pass. The sheer expanse of mountains seen from there is awe-inspiring, but perhaps most impressive are two particular tooth-like peaks that serrate the skyline—Uncompahgre and Wetterhorn. Naturally, Uncompahgre, being the higher of the pair, has received most of the attention, but surely Wetterhorn is a spectacular mountain in its own right and one of the more challenging Fourteeners to climb.

Wetterhorn Peak (sometimes simply called the Wetterhorn) rises to 14,015´ above the upper basins of Matterhorn Creek, East Cimarron River, and Wetterhorn Creek. All three basins were carved by ancient glaciers, and as each glacier ground in a separate direction, they left a single high point between them now called the Wetterhorn. Though the glaciers are now vanished, the alpine basins they scooped out are wonderful backpacking destinations for those who enjoy camping away from the crowd.

The Wetterhorn was named in 1874 by William Marshall of the Wheeler Survey. Often following on the heels of their friendly competition, the Hayden Survey, many of the place names given by the Wheeler men did not survive. Wetterhorn, however, is an exception. During

Marshall's climb of Uncompahgre on August 29, 1874, he wrote: "The Wetterhorn, to the south of west a few miles from Uncompahgre Peak, is a shark's nose in form, and its ascent being unnecessary for topographical purposes, was not attempted. It exceeds 14,000 in altitude and appears inaccessible."

Marshall named the peak after a famous Swiss peak, and from certain angles—particularly the upper East Cimarron basin—there is a degree of resemblance between them. Marshall's judgement of the peak appearing inaccessible, though, would be disproved thirty-two years later when D. Utter, George C. Barnard, C. Smedley, and W. P. Smedley climbed it via its south ridge. That ascent made Wetterhorn among the last dozen or so Fourteeners to be climbed, and it remains one of the most challenging peaks in the eastern San Juans.

Though thousands have climbed the Wetterhorn since that foursome in 1906, it is not a peak for novice mountaineers. Those used to the gentle grades and well-marked paths on Uncompahgre and Handies will find Wetterhorn a very different sort of peak. Wetterhorn requires extensive use of hands and feet on its upper 500 feet, slopes are very steep in places, and loose gravel can make footing treacherous. Although it is not a peak requiring ropes and technical climbing gear, route-finding skills, good balance and a lack of acrophobia are necessities on Wetterhorn. With these skills and its generally sound rock, many find Wetterhorn an exhilarating ascent. Be certain, though, to start early and allow a full day for the climb.

For the nontechnical climber, the south ridge route on Wetterhorn is *the* route on the peak. From Capitol City, drive up the North Henson Creek Road for two miles nearly to the crossing of Matterhorn Creek. Here, a four-wheel drive road branches to the right for another .5 miles to a good parking area at 10,700′. Even for those not interested in climbing the peak, a hike from here into the Matterhorn basin is a relatively easy and gorgeous day hike. The trail climbs steadily, following Matterhorn Creek's mineral-tinged waters, and enters a large park at

11,000´. A fine campsite is found in the upper portion of this park, and following the westerly stream fork here leads to an unnamed green basin visited by few except shepherds and their sheep.

The main trail makes two long switchbacks climbing out of the park, but a large buttress blocks the view of Wetterhorn until timberline is reached at about 11,800´. At this point, 13,590´ Matterhorn (less aptly named than Wetterhorn) dominates the view directly ahead, along with a long serrated ridge leading west from it to Wetterhorn.

Once at timberline, continue along the trail to a level area at about 12,200', to the foot of the slopes of Matterhorn. From here, follow the marked trail across the grassy expanse west toward the small basin on Wetterhorn's east flank.

Once in the flat basin area at 12,800´ (obvious on the Wetterhorn Peak Quadrangle) head southwest on the trail to the saddle at 13,100´. Nearly any good hiker who is acclimated can make it to this point, and should consider doing so, since a dramatic view suddenly opens up here to the western San Juans. Mount Wilson and Wilson Peak are especially prominent on the western skyline, and from a bit farther up the ridge, the sharp pyramid of Mount Sneffels becomes visible. Far below you may hear and see hundreds of grazing sheep, which look from this vantage point like white mushrooms in the alpine meadows. Nearer to you, even at your feet, look for the creamy white goblets of arctic gentians and perhaps even a high-flying broad-tailed hummingbird.

This saddle on the south ridge pretty well ends the "pedestrian trail" on the peak, for just above the hump I call Gold Hill, the ridge becomes very rocky. From here, it will be necessary to climb with both hands and feet, and though the route is fairly well marked with rock cairns, it is not a place for those timid of heights or who are not confident climbing on rocks. At about 13,400′, the route passes to the west side of the ridge, ascending a particularly gravelly couloir before reaching better rock. Climb slowly in this couloir, making sure of good footing and paying close attention to the cairns.

At 13,750′, the route reaches the top of the ridge again and climbs around the east side of a fifty-foot high shark's tooth, an obvious landmark from afar. In the notch between the tooth and the main peak, the route climbs an eight-foot ledge, then drops down a smooth slab a few feet to the foot of the final pitch: 150 feet of good handholds and footholds to the summit. If you make it to the base of the final pitch, you can probably make it the rest of the distance, for the rock is sound, though steep and a bit exposed.

The summit of Wetterhorn is surprisingly level and more surprisingly, home to a number of marmots and panhandling chipmunks! Sign the summit register and enjoy the spectacular view, but don't tarry too long. Lightning can be a threat here, and you'll need to allow plenty of time to climb down the tricky portions. Be careful to descend the same route as you ascended, or you could wind up in some very hazardous terrain.

When you're safely back in Lake City, consider finishing the day with a drive to Windy Point to watch the sunset. Wetterhorn will be there, piercing the red-orange sky, but now you'll see it with a satisfaction that only climbers know. In a small way, for a day, the "inaccessible" Wetterhorn was yours.

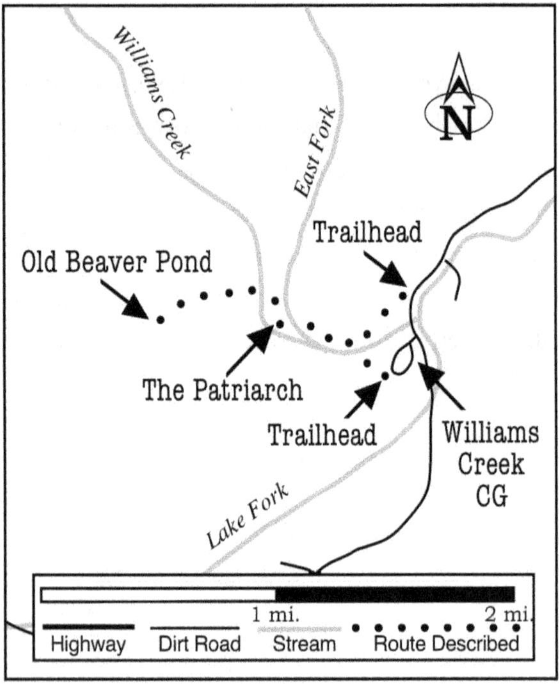
Williams Creek
East Fork
Trailhead
Old Beaver Pond
The Patriarch
Trailhead
Williams
Creek
CG
Lake Fork
1 mi.
2 mi.
Highway
Dirt Road
Stream
Route Described

18 Williams Creek

Sometimes I'm asked, "Where's a good place near Lake City to go on a short hike with my family? Not too long, though, we've only got a couple of hours." For those on a limited time schedule, and who would rather not ford icy streams and scale steep mountainsides, I know of few finer short hikes in the Lake City area than the Williams Creek Trail.

The Williams Creek Trail has two possible beginning points. The "official trailhead" is well marked and leaves County Road 30 not far past the entrance of the former Camp Redcloud, about nine miles from Lake City. The second leaves from the far end of the Williams Creek Forest Service Campground loop, a bit father up the road. From the official marked trailhead on County Road 30, the trail immediately enters a long hidden meadow that offers great views behind you to "The Backbone of North America," the Continental Divide. The rugged north side of the Divide is quite impressive.

Beyond the flat meadow, you'll climb a short steep hill and will be in an open stand of ponderosa pines, somewhat rare this far up the Lake Fork Valley. The trail soon passes the fenced Williams Creek Campground water supply. Continuing upstream and after crossing the East Fork of Williams Creek, the trail traverses a grassy hillside.

Not far along the side hill trail, you'll come upon the location of what was once one of the highlights of Williams Creek, a triple-trunked Douglas fir I called "The Patriarch." Most trees are impressive because of their height; The Patriarch was impressive because of its roots. The most massive segments of the Patriarch's root system are well exposed, stretching downhill across the trail, and far uphill as well. One can only guess how far underground these sinews stretch.

[Author's 2007 note: Alas, even Patriarchs are mortal. Sometime during the late 1990s, most of the Patriarch tumbled to the ground in a windstorm. Its amazing roots remain in place, however, a fine remnant of this landmark fir.]

A few hundred yards above The Patriarch, the trail crosses Williams Creek at a bend in the canyon where cliffs and spires of volcanic rock jut overhead. From here the trail climbs up a nameless, mostly-dry tributary. This is the steepest portion of the trail, so take your time. You may notice that you are not the only one who uses this trail; sign from elk and coyote is particularly abundant. Also, especially in the morning, keep an eye out for juncos, chickadees, and Townsend's solitaires. Climbing the side hill above this nameless fork is a great place to observe the effects of aspect on vegetation. The trail side of the valley is a southern exposure, and supports only grasses and smell plants. It appears nearly desert-like. Just across the small valley, however, on the northern exposure, grows a dense forest of Englemann spruce. One April I noticed a small daisy in full bloom on the south slope, while less than fifty yards away, the north slope was still buried in mid-winter under two feet of snow!

After the side hill levels off a bit, you'll suddenly come upon a small meadow filled with the remnants of a once-impressive beaver pond. The beavers have long left the valley, and now a mountain meadow is in the process of filling in the pond. This meadow is a good destination for those with limited time, and the trail is not as well-maintained beyond that point. If you hike that far, you will have done about 1.25 miles and will have climbed about 600 feet. You may, however, want to hike a short distance further on the trail to the large rock talus slope and see if you can catch a glimpse of the high country's rock-dwellers, the marmot or pika.

Are you short on time, but long on desire for a family hike in the high country? Spend a morning or afternoon up Williams Creek … and receive an excellent, easy introduction to the joys of Lake City hiking.

www.ingramcontent.com/pod-product-compliance
Lightning Source LLC
Chambersburg PA
CBHW060303050426
42448CB00009B/1736